A BOY FROM GLASGOW STREET

Norman Pascoe

A BOY FROM GLASGOW STREET

NORMAN PASCOE

© Norman Pascoe, 2014

Published by Easter Morn Publishing

www.nowty999@gmail.com

A CIP catalogue record for this book is available from the British Library.

ISBN 978-0-9929563-0-1

Book layout and cover design by Clare Brayshaw

Prepared and printed by:

York Publishing Services Ltd
64 Hallfield Road
Layerthorpe
York YO31 7ZQ

Tel: 01904 431213

Website: www.yps-publishing.co.uk

PROLOGUE

This story is about a working class boy, his attempt to follow a dream on little money and doing what he had to do achieving it. The adventures along the way, his enriched childhood in the 1950's when children left home in the morning, returning when hungry or darkness fell. Times when children roamed freely exploring, climbed trees and cliffs, taking risks, loving the freedom. Wrongdoing earned them a cuff around the ears from the local bobby. Front doors were left unlocked, neighbours were trusted, everybody knew everyone's business, and in times of adversity rallied round to help those less fortunate.

The different types of historical boats he fished, even an old tug they used for towing newly built navy destroyers and nuclear submarines around Barrow docks. The necessity of having to convert the tug into a stern trawler after the contract in the docks finished unexpectedly. This skilled work normally carried out in a shipyard being arranged by three young lads on a limited budget. They and their beloved boat with the tall funnel were the laughing stock of the fishing harbours around the Irish Sea. Over time the Melanie Jane proved herself over and over again. They were involved in the rescue of a coaster's crew during a severe storm that was carried out in treacherous conditions as darkness fell, risking their lives to save others. The salvage of the trawler Stephil sunk off Walney Island and the various near misses when caught out in dangerous situations. Norm's innocent attempts attracting the opposite sex are hilarious. His love of boating and fishing shines through always. Trying so very hard to make a living from the unforgiving sea.

He had a period where he worked as a painting and decorating supervisor for the Job Creation scheme. This entailed driving sixteen year old boys and girls from the most deprived areas around the most beautiful areas of the Cumbrian Lake District, these children had no formal qualifications and neither had Norm! Painting and decorating outward bound schools, village halls plus a million miles of metal railings for the National Trust, their head quarters a hire van! The adventures and scrapes they got him into were hilarious. Some of these kids were punk rockers who turned out to be right characters. Enough adventures for a follow on book, perhaps?

After a spell as senior supervisor over several teams in Cumbria the government schemes finished, Norm was back to job hunting. After getting married he began working down the sewers to earn the money to open a successful village shop, selling groceries and fresh fish. The call of the sea was too strong the shop was sold. Norm became skipper of a hydrographic survey boat charting the safe passage of the new generation of Trident submarines from the port of Barrow. Also becoming skipper of a pilot boat just like his lifelong friend George, guiding ships safely into harbour in storms and calms.

A snap of two of the grandchildren playing on the beach outside of their remote cottage taken with a cheap 'Argos' camera won a Sunday Express major photography competition. The prize a long holiday touring to all the best safari parks in Kenya, including Tree Tops, all expenses paid. The icing on the cake for Norm was having his winning photo on the front cover of the Sunday Express magazine! The photos he took on safari earned him an enrolment of a Licentiate of the Royal Photographic Society of Great Britain which bought a tear to his wife's eye. Pauline had sent the snap in against Norm's wishes! This win gave Norm the incentive to carry on with his new hobby, winning many more competitions having photos published in books and calendars. He sold many of his Cumbrian sheep in the snow Christmas cards for the local hospice. On his trip to Kenya he met a lovely couple who became instant friends, his new friend Richard was an author who has written over sixty books and only later in their friendship revealed he was a Lord. Norm had to take early retirement on medical grounds, which is hardly surprising when you read the book. He spends his time transferring all his thousands of photographs onto free web sites dedicated to people who like him love everything maritime worldwide, receiving over three million hits on 'trawler photos' site. Always assisted and encouraged by his long suffering wife Pauline, lovely stepchildren and their families.

ACKNOWLEDGEMENTS

A big thank you goes to my lifelong friend's Brian and Stewart two resourceful, loyal shipmates who shared some great adventures with me. Grateful thanks to my late sisters Lillian and Jean who introduced me to my beautiful wife Pauline nearly forty years ago. A day does not go by without me thinking about you. My five wonderful stepchildren for welcoming me so warmly into their lives, my life certainly changed for the better. Also our ten grandchildren, plus five great grandchildren, they brighten up our lives. The volunteers in Duddon Inshore Rescue lifeboat, they give up their precious time risking their lives to save others around our dangerous local shores. A donation from each book sold will go to this local charity to help buy some much needed new equipment. Hopefully somebody will buy the book besides my friends and a few lassies in Pauline's line dancing class! Not forgetting our best friend's Glenys and Dave who bought our lovely cottage, (I did tell you it was prone to flooding). They listened to all my tales and encouraged me to put it all down to paper. Thank you for all the work put into the book by Duncan and the ace team at YPS publishing for all their professional work and guidance.

Last but not least my lovely wife Pauline who has always been my rock in good times and bad, I cannot for one moment imagine my life without you by my side. You already know how much I love you!

Some names have been changed to save any embarrassment.

CHAPTER ONE

My name is Norm I was born into an overcrowded tiny terraced house in a place called Barrow-in-Furness, Lancashire (now called Cumbria). There is a good chance you will not have heard of Barrow it being on the end of a long cul-de-sac near the Lake District. When you look at a map of England we are on the northwest corner, the Irish Sea on our western side adjacent to the Isle of Man. Inland are the beautiful mountains of the Lake District easily accessible to us. A short walk in any direction will give a glorious view of the Lakeland mountains from anywhere in our town. Barrows claim to fame was the steelworks and Vickers shipyard building ocean liners, tankers, warships and nuclear submarines, now we only build submarines and have no steelworks. Barrow is sheltered from the strong westerly gales by Walney Island connected to Barrow by Jubilee Bridge. Walney is about eleven miles long, a mile wide with very narrow bits which in major westerly storms combining with spring tides nearly cut the island into two. There is a lighthouse on the southern tip and nature reserves at either ends. Walney Island provides the shelter to launch newly built ships and submarines into the channel also a long safe approach into Barrow docks.

I was born in 59 Glasgow Street unfortunately in great pain because of a huge growth on the base of my spine. The doctor said I needed to be sent to hospital immediately for an operation to remove it, telling my mother to expect the worst. This was the year 1950 and little was known of this particular medical problem. Dad borrowed a pram from a neighbour and pushed me the short distance to North Lonsdale Hospital. I had an operation which left me to grow up with permanent back pain including among other things curvature of the spine. Much to the surprise of my family I survived, returning back home. Mum had nine children but unfortunately lost two babies who both died soon after birth.

I shared a box-room with my two elder brothers sleeping in one bed, an arrangement we always hated. Our only bedroom furniture being an orange box on which sat a candle, the room was too small for anything else. The house was lit by gas mantles but owing to lack of money the mantles were never renewed upstairs. Mum and dad had the middle bedroom with the only wardrobe, a wardrobe being of no use to us brothers, possessing no spare change of clothing anyway. At bed time we chucked our clothes on the floor by the bed sleeping naked possessing no pyjamas. The four girls had the largest bedroom sharing one bed. Every bed had a pee-pot (as my mother would call them) underneath, which all had to be carried carefully downstairs each morning to be emptied in the back yard toilet. Toilet paper being newspapers cut into squares and hung on a nail behind the door, a small oil lamp was lit in winter to stop the cistern freezing up. With nine people having to use one toilet we boys would often resort to using the drain in the back yard to pee in.

When we crowded in at meal times and asked mum what are we having for dinner? Mum would invariably say "Shit with sugar on!" In those days just after the war feeding a large family posed a huge problem, money was very tight, we always felt hungry. Mum would send one of us to the bakery to ask if there were any stale cakes left over or the fruit shop to ask about any damaged fruit going spare. You could not afford to be proud in those days when hungry and poor! Dad was always on a manual workers wage which did not stretch far and he relied on occasional overtime work. Food was bought every day for a large family like ours because nothing was ever left over after a meal. We were like a swarm of locust. Potatoes were our main staple diet, chipped, boiled, roasted or mashed. Huge quantities were consumed usually served with beans or eggs, with plenty of bread and butter. Mum must have thought she had sired magicians her cooking disappeared so quickly. We had no fridge to keep anything fresh, so in hot weather in particular any fish caught were filleted and eaten for the next meal, likewise snared rabbits.

Winkles picked at Biggar Bank beach provided us with iron even though it was a long walk from Glasgow Street to collect them. Dad would give us a bucket then a gang of us would set off on our trek to Walney Island. If it was a very low tide a nice bonus was to find half a dozen eating crabs. After bringing them home the winkles were put in mum's oldest pan and boiled on the stove. Shortly after a row of small children would sit in our back street and using bent pins prise the meat from the still hot shells. Looking in the windows of the lovely timbered café on the island we could see the lucky families sitting with their tea and cakes. We always wished we had the money for an ice cream cone or sweets. Luckily there were public drinking fountains on the shore front where we could slake our thirst. There were two open air pools, one for sailing model yachts and swimming, the other shallow for the younger children to paddle. One day my youngest sister fell into the deeper pool, she was drowning a young man jumped in and pulled her out. This hero without question saved her life. The poor girl walked all the way back home soaked to the skin, her dress clinging to her body, crying, still in shock but alive. Dad gave her a good hiding when he found out what happened.

The downstairs parlour had a coal fire only used if we had special visitors and later for courting couples. The middle room was dominated by a blacked iron coal range with an oven and huge kettle which was forever steaming away. An old second hand sofa dominated the room, plus a split leather armchair with the stuffing hanging out where dad always sat his pipe rack within easy reach. My brothers used to smirk when asking for a half ounce of 'Shag' at the corner shop for dad's pipe. Four chairs around a scrubbed pine table covered with news paper during the week, Sunday we used a tablecloth. Always on the table were salt, pepper, vinegar, sauce bottle, butter-dish and milk in a bottle.

Lino covered the floorboards under which very big cockroaches lived roaming about in the dark, it was not pleasant to feel the crunch when you stepped on one. We also had plenty of mice which the cat loved to chase around the house. We lads used to laugh at the girls and mum when a mouse ran across the room, just like in the comics. The ladies screamed and stood on the nearest chair lifting up their skirts they were absolutely petrified! Of course we found this was hilarious taking our time to catch the mouse. I always felt sorry for the mice it was the cockroaches that I detested.

The problem of the vermin was only solved when dad put his foot through the rotten floor boards and promptly fell flat on his face. Then he had us rip up all the downstairs floorboards cutting them up for firewood.

Afterwards we concreted all the ground floor rooms mixing it all by hand in our backyard. It was a long time before we could afford lino down on our newly cemented floors, but there was a rather pleasing pattern of cat paw prints all over the surface. Dad locked us all out of the house until the cement went off, accidently locking the two cats indoors for the day. Mother's two cats never knew how lucky they were not to be strangled. Dad was well pissed off when he saw the paw prints they had made lovely patterns in the wet cement! We ended up with a smack for laughing but it was worth it! With all the material nicked from the Corporation Yard depot, even the shovels, dad never had to pay a penny for the job.

The kitchen eventually had a gas cooker with a small gas geyser to heat a small amount of hot water over the Belfast sink. Coal was kept in the kitchen under the stairs saving us going into the back yard at night in bad weather. One day someone gave dad a proper full size bath, he installed it in the kitchen. We only used it once because mother complained it took up too much room. Also it took far too long to fill up with buckets, typically dad did not think to plumb it in. So it was covered in heavy wooden boards for her to use as a kitchen worktop. Then it was back to using the big zinc bath that hung on a nail in the backyard. I was the youngest in the family the oldest was sixteen, on the rare occasion we had a bath night the zinc bath was carried in front of the fire. This was laboriously filled up with buckets of hot water, which I helped mum to carry. I would look at the clean soapy water with longing knowing that the eldest would be first, the youngest last. When it was finally my turn it looked like mushroom soup! I swear that I was cleaner going in than coming out!

My right leg is longer than the left leg causing me to walk with a limp, my left foot is several sizes bigger than the right foot so one foot fitted snugly into one shoe and the other was loose inside the other shoe. Mum solved my problem by stuffing in newspaper to fill the gap in my shoe. My brothers used to laugh telling me I had somebody else's leg! Mum never had the time or the inclination to bother with hospital appointments with me, nowadays of course this would never happen, babies are closely monitored from birth. Having carried nine children mum was tired having a struggle to feed everybody without worrying about me. I was determined to keep up with my mates and not be seen to be different in any way. Mum was I can safely say a little on the eccentric side!

Dad met my mum working on farm service he was an orphan a tough hard man, ruling the house by fear. I was sixteen years of age before being confidant enough to stand up to him. We seemed to rub along better then calling a truce. After getting married they managed a farm but after the first child was born moved to Barrow for the chance of higher wages. They eventually rented this house in Glasgow Street for years. The corporation yard was only across our street so dad found it handy for work. He drove and looked after a steam roller during the war, then ran the tarmac plant under the arches of Greengate Street bridge. The yard covered several acres, the stables were still intact but horses had given way to motor vehicles. I must have been only four when mum sent me over the road to take dad his billycan with loose tea mixed with sugar, also a packet of jam sandwiches for his lunch. He would eat under the bridge arches, where the workmen would sit by the big pot bellied coke stove to have dinner. While dad filled up the corporation wagons with tarmac or chippings using the bright yellow loading shovel, I would play for hours amongst the huge piles of lime stone chippings. The yard foreman did not mind me roaming around all the workmen were very friendly. Only shouting at me when I climbed on to the loading shovel and started up the diesel engine then trying my hardest to reach the clutch pedal to drive it away!

Dad never could afford to give us any pocket money, his wages were poor and overtime was hard to come by. Never having access to sweets when young explains my teeth being so good in later life, something to be grateful for.

One winter in the early hours of the morning when we were all tucked up in bed there was a banging on the door, poor dad was called out to help grit the roads. Into our bedroom dad came to collect his heavy ex army greatcoat off our bed leaving us freezing. There was frost on the inside and the outside of the windows. My brothers and I would stand shivering at our bedroom window watching dad climb onto the back of a lorry loaded with rock salt, driving off down the road chucking shovel after shovel of grit out as the lorry slowly drove along. At breakfast a quick hot drink and porridge then he was back to work, grateful for the night's overtime.

Tatters used to call around the back streets and shout "Rags, bones old iron" at the tops of their voices, they would say to me "Run in and ask your mother if you have any old rags? Mum would send me out to answer "I am wearing them!" One tramp in particular pushed a handcart around with colourful balloons attached. The old lady next door would bring him a mug of tea and a piece of fruitcake. This man had a wonderful operatic voice and would sing like Mario Lanza. It was rumoured that he was an educated man who fell on hard times turning to drink. This was my first experience of classical music all those many years ago.

We had a big surprise waking up one morning in December our bedroom seemed a lot brighter, peering out of the bedroom window showed all our drab smoked stained houses appearing lovely under a mantle of pristine white snow. My brothers and I could not wait to throw on our clothes it was much too cold to wash. Rushing to eat our porridge mum said the school would not be open snow being up to our kitchen window ledge. I have never seen snow that deep before or since. Dad had already been called out to grit the roads and clear snow hours earlier. We had no wellingtons so had to use our only pair of shoes in the deep snow, the cardboard inside the shoe used to cover the holes in the sole soon got soggy. Big brother soon solved the problem, he borrowed the scissors and cut some lino from behind the armchair and made us some waterproof soles to put inside our shoes instead of cardboard. I was so proud of him! No gloves, scarves or hats but what you have never had you do not miss mother said "I don't want you boys growing up soft." We kids thought there was no bloody chance of that happening! Our first chore was to make a path down to the toilet at the bottom of our long backyard, the snow being three feet deep. We loved every minute of digging through the snow. Next job was the snow drift at our front door then onto our neighbour's house knowing they were too old and frail to manage it themselves. Some of them brought us out toast and tea we felt very grown up. Any house that did not possess any shovels asked us to clear their snow away. We started to get payment which mother soon relieved us of.

We were all cold and exhausted at the end of that first day of the snow fall, our fingers were blue with cold the pain when thawing out our hands by the fire was excruciating. Our legs were blue up to our knees with being in deep snow wearing only shoes. The rooms in the house were always very cold the only fire lit was in the middle room. When the wet clothes were put in front to dry very little heat penetrated to the rest of the room, even the clothes rack that hung from the ceiling was always full of wet clothes. My memory of those winters was of being perpetually cold day and night it was the only time that I was glad of having the warmth of two brothers sharing my bed. Everybody seemed to be coughing and blowing their noses. Two green candles were always running from our nostrils the sleeves on our jumpers were in use continuously to wipe our noses. Sometimes I would daydream about having enough coal to have all the rooms in the house with the fires lit, banked up blazing away not having to eke out the coal.

Our friend's father made a heavy wooden sledge a gang of us would pull this all the way to Furness Abbey where the hill was very steep. This was a meeting place then as now for all the local children. We sped down the hill at break neck speeds always one of our gang would sprain or break something ensuring a trip to hospital to round off an exciting day. Wet, tired and hungry we would stay until dark then reluctantly make our way home.

Coal deliveries were not getting through the roads were cut off by huge drifts, so dad sent us with our barrow to collect a load of coke from the gasworks taking all three of us lads to push it back through the deep snow. All the children in our street decided to build the mother of all snow forts in our back street that would last for a long time. The walls were three feet thick big enough to have a room to sit in complete with shelf to hold a candle. This fort was the envy of all the other street gangs who raided us regularly ensuring vicious snowball fights. They were not averse to having put a stone inside their snowballs. We sat inside our little fort at night with the light from our candle until called in by our mothers to get ready for bed. After several freezing days the snow fort turned into ice hard as stone, impossible to destroy. The fort was still there when the thaw came and all the streets snow had melted. Then it froze even harder our house had frost and ice inside as well as the outside of the windows.

In the summer dad had been given a piano off somebody in the pub, he had it installed in our parlour to make us look posh he said, what a laugh. Mum polished it every day we would get a smack if we scratched it or attempted to play it. We were amazed when dad told my brothers to manhandle it into the back yard one particularly cold morning. Passing us a sledge hammer he told us to smash it into little pieces. Saying "the piano has to go we have nothing else to burn!" What fun we had wielding that big hammer but feeling sad, it seemed like vandalism. Mother was upset it was her pride and joy, pity we did not know anybody who knew how to play one. The piano did not die in vain it kept us warm for a while I for one was grateful, shame about all the beatings we had received for playing on it.

Everyone in our house received a stocking at Christmas containing an apple, orange and nuts. We had one present each containing a game such as Ludo, Draughts, Snakes and ladders, Dominoes, Hangman or a set of playing cards for the long dark nights. Mum always stored them on top of her wardrobe we would always rip a corner of paper wrapping to see what we had, then on the special morning regret being so nosy! The rare Christmas we had a selection box each my brothers had been on top of the wardrobe weeks earlier very carefully slipping out most of the chocolate then resealing them. That was a bit of a bummer on Christmas morning.

We were not sad when the thaw came life was hard enough without having to endure adverse weather conditions for so long. These long winter nights in a cold house made me want to go to bed early to keep warm, I read by the light of my candle perched on top of our bed side table or upturned orange box to be accurate. My favourite books being Treasure Island, Robinson Crusoe, indeed anything I could get my hands on.

My dad often sent us brothers to bed early for being naughty telling us not to come downstairs on pain of death. We would be desperate for a pee and mum had not yet brought up the pee pots. None of us dared to go downstairs to the toilet so we decided to all pee out of the front bedroom window. My eldest brother lifted the bottom of the sash window unfortunately it was rotten. Then he leaned on it the full window crashing to the ground followed closely by him "I think my fucking legs broken" he shouted. Dad came rushing out of the front door shouting "You bloody kids will be the death of me" and dashed off to find a pram to wheel him up to the hospital. In the meantime we helped carry the debris away, a kind neighbour blanked off the hole where the bedroom window used to be. Big brother was right "It was fucking broken!" We all kept out of dad's way for a few days. Somehow it seemed no matter how hard we tried we kept getting on the wrong side of our dad making him even worse tempered. Sitting in front of the fire one night having a drawing competition with my brothers, I thought of drawing dad. Thinking he might be pleased and show me some affection? This was a bad idea when told it was a portrait of him he gave me a bloody good hiding, calling me a cheeky little bastard. No more illusions of being an artist for a while after that episode.

We worked an allotment off Friars lane dad was a great gardener growing all kinds of produce to help feed his large family. His butcher's bike had a box on the front to carry garden produce or me if I was lucky. Mum was a good cook, rhubarb or apple pies disappeared as fast as they were baked. Her speciality was a fresh cream trifle which was placed on the outside window sill to set and keep cool. A plate on top kept the soot off and the cats away from the cream. This was before we owned a refrigerator. One day walking into the kitchen I received a smack off mother. "What was that for Mum?" I asked.

"For sticking your fingers in my trifle you greedy little sod!"

On this rare occasion I was innocent receiving an apology when mum saw our tom cat pushing the plate to one side with his paw, then licking off the cream. Clever cat setting me up to take the rap!

We were always feeling hungry and overcrowded, always falling out with each other not like the Waltons in any way that is for sure. We played hunt the bed bugs and picked the fleas off the cats, I was always a bit pongy with dribbling in my trousers often, mum washed my only pair of short pants on a Sunday night so having to go to bed early that's when I developed my love of books. A lovely old lady in our street lent me hundreds over the years.

When our parents were out of the house for an hour or two some of our friends in the street would pile into our house, drag the mattresses off our beds throwing them to the bottom of the stairs to play parachutist. We all took turns jumping from the bedroom landing. Great fun until we had to drag them all back up the stairs again, putting them back before our parents came home. Playing football in the biggest bedroom was good fun when home alone until the next door neighbours complained to dad about living next door to a zoo! We played in our back street, boys and girls joining in playing marbles, hop scotch, catch one kiss one, a game where we all received our first kisses. Hide and seek using the nearby streets in the dark. The dares where you knocked on front doors then run away into the darkness. Or sometimes two front doors were tied together with a length of rope then watching the chaos from a safe distance. Putting up makeshift tents in the back street using a clothes horse and blankets off somebody's bed was popular. A craze at one time of tying a bean can to the bottom of our feet with string making a loud clanking noise when walking. Using two cans with a tightly stretched string between them made a phone enabling two friends to talk. We spent hours playing on our friend's wooden stilts made by his dad. When older we would orchard raid travelling to Manor farm climbing over the high sand stone wall, sometimes getting caught by the farmer earning us a clip around our ears.

Making bows and arrows was a fad at one time it ensured one of us would be taken to North Lonsdale Hospital to have an arrow removed from our body. One of the kids used to fire flaming arrows into the night sky from his bedroom window after becoming obsessed with cowboy and Indian films, until his dad coming home from the pub caught him in the act one night. That lad became an upstanding member of our community! Goal posts were chalked on back street walls and five a side football was popular, always cricket in the summer, some dads would play out with us after tea, not ours though. We were never bored did not know what that word meant, happy in our various gangs getting up to mischief but never ever committed vandalism. Nobody ever locked their doors and it was many years later that my mother started to lock her front door at night.

Occasionally we would run past the fruit shop very fast grabbing one apple each from the boxes on display outside on the pavement. Barrow Park was well used by the local lads who knew where all the best conker and crab apple trees were located. Our favourite pastime was on the huge park lake hiring out a paddle boat, then graduating to the sleek varnished rowing boats. The boathouse was a magical place always having clinker built rowing boats out for repairs, the smell of varnish lingering and the strong smell of glue. The big lads used to abandon the boats usually with a hole in the bottom, running off hotly pursued by the Park Keeper. There were long queues waiting to get a ticket to hire these boats in good weather, mostly it was a rare treat for four of us to afford a boat for one hour. If somebody we knew had a rowing boat on hire, we stood on one of the two bridges that the boats had to pass under and jumped off the bridge into the back of the boat. The occupants would nearly die of shock when this happened with the boat nearly capsizing. I only missed the back of the boat once ending up in water above my waist, giving the occupants of the boat a great laugh! When the Park Keepers had enough of escorting us to the park gates they would ban us for a time.

The older lads in our street went after rabbits using snares or ferrets to catch them, a very welcome addition to our dinner tables. Bank lines with fifty hooks baited with lugworm were set on the shore to catch flounders. Mussels and cockles which were in abundance on the sands of Morecambe bay these were regularly collected, boiled with a little pepper and vinegar added they tasted divine. When we had a few spare fish or a rabbit, mum always made sure that I took it to any old person living on their own that were worse off than us, also making sure we cleaned away any snow for them in winter. Mum made sure that we were always available to do any odd jobs for neighbours relieving us of any money received. A good sense of community everybody in the same boat keeping an eye on each other. Summer was mushroom picking time the back end of the year was spent picking rose hips along the old railway line. The disused tracks ran from Salthouse to Rampside a good place for the rose hip and blackberry bushes to grow. We took them to get weighed at a shop on Rawlinson Street they were used to make rose hip syrup. All our pennies from this hard work went to help feed our family.

One game that never died out was collecting conkers after school. Roaming far and wide into the woods we found the best trees to climb. A hole was put through the centre of the conker and string or a bootlace put through. The more conkers you smashed of the opponents the more famous your conker became. Cheats soaked them in vinegar and baked them to make sure they were extra hard.

Mum smoked Woodbines daily until the age of seventy, (when the doctor told her to give up she did, chucking all her cigarettes onto the fire).

She would walk around the house doing her chores with a lit cigarette in her mouth, the length of ash growing ever longer. We would sit around the kitchen table waiting for mum to bring in our plates of egg and chips, having a bet on who would have the dubious pleasure of her two inches of fag ash on their plate. If you had the temerity to point out the line of grey ash spread across your otherwise pristine egg, you would receive a slap across your head and mum would tell you not to be so bloody fussy!

Coming home from school at lunch time feeling very hungry, sometimes the only thing to eat was two slices of bread each and a scoop of dripping fat out of the frying pan, ignoring the neat mice footprints running across the pan. One day at school the teacher said "put your hand up anyone who can draw any animal footprints." Feeling very important I strode to the blackboard and chalked a row of mice footprints, it was very annoying when the teacher and my class mates started laughing! Other times a dish of cold porridge we were delighted to see had been left from the previous breakfast, a spoonful of jam in the middle, and off back to school. All of us were looking forward to a cooked meal at tea time.

We were all pleased when dad had electricity installed in the downstairs rooms he did not have enough money to have it all done at once, so we still had gas lighting upstairs. Candles were still in use in the bedrooms as the delicate gas mantles were too expensive to replace. This was fair enough it was us that bust the mantles playing pillow fights on the bed. Mum bought our first fridge on weekly payments and to help to make it pay sent us combing the streets for used lolly sticks. She washed and reused them for making her own ice lollies selling to local kids "Every little helps!" mum would say.

Most of our corner shop owners were very nice but one a couple of streets away was a right mean and miserable sod. One of our gang came to tell us that this particular shop keeper was selling chocolate Easter eggs at less than half price. This was three weeks before Christmas so obviously it was old stock. We all clubbed together getting enough money for two eggs to share between us, gave the man his money very pleased thinking what a real bargain. Sitting in our friends shed we tore off the box and foil wrapping only to discover the first egg was full of cockroaches busily eating the chocolate. The next egg was a funny grey colour but did not contain any insects, even we realised it was inedible. Back to the shop we marched to get our money back, only to be told that he would not give us a refund we would have to buy something else. He stood behind his counter the usual large dewdrop hanging from the end of his nose, telling us to hurry up or get out. Pointing to the glass fronted biscuit tins I asked for the equivalent refund in broken biscuits. He leaned over to open the tin giving me the opportunity to give him the 'V' sign behind his back. Unfortunately he saw my reflection in the glass fronted biscuit tin, then turning around so quickly for an elderly man smacked me right between my eyes, he shouted "You cheeky little bastard!" It is true about seeing stars when hit hard in your face, moments later the three of us were kicked out of the shop the door slamming shut behind us. My friend said what did you upset him for Norm now we have nothing! After telling my friend's dad about the rotten Easter eggs he was all for going to the shop to sort the man out and get our money back, until he noticed my black eye asking how I received it. He told us to put it all down to experience.

When it snowed we used our stolen shovels from the corporation yard and cleared snow off pavements, throwing the snow into the road edge, no cars in our street in those days. Carol singing door to door also bought some welcome pennies. Bonfire night was a big occasion for our gang collecting old furniture, car tyres, wood and any old stuff people wanted rid of. Weeks ahead we stockpiled all our accumulated treasure and needed a rota of guards making sure rival gangs did not raid our wood. Some of the bonfires were lit early by jealous gangs. Many bonfires were huge even ours in Glasgow Street set fire to several back yard doors, windows were cracking with the heat. The fire brigade were called out much to our annoyance! The next day the council lorry would come around to clear up the mess left. Shops stocked fireworks very early we saved to buy large quantities of penny bangers setting them off weeks too soon, receiving many a clip around your ears from the local bobby. Additional money was obtained by wheeling a straw stuffed Guy Fawkes around the outside of pub doorways in an old pram, if lucky a drunk coming out would be overly generous. We asked for a penny for the Guy trying to target young courting couples. The young man not wanting to appear mean in front of his girlfriend would begrudgingly be generous. All these tricks were passed on from the older boys who had grown out of doing it.

To avoid the police we went down the old line to set off fireworks, this railway line used to connect Salthouse to Roa Island in the former days when a ferry service went from the pier at Roa Island. The railway lines had all been removed it now made an excellent flat path to cycle or walk down. By the coal fired power station is a Second World War pill box where we used to take turns to man it while the other members of our gang would storm the pill box, hurling penny bangers through the firing slits pretending they were grenades. Screaming war cry's at the tops of our voices, many a burn was received but we had good fun! One day going down the old line by the sidings at Salt house paper mill, we found a yellow substance that one of the older lads recognised as sulphur from his chemistry lessons. He informed us that when lit, it burned and bubbled giving off a bad egg smell, when inhaled it caused light headiness and feelings of being drunk. We lit up mounds of the stuff staggering around high as a kite. This explains my memory loss and constant migraines. Or it could be the competitions between us to see who could bite the heads off lead toy soldiers the fastest.

Our parents let us run wild, we all left home early in the morning and returned when hunger set in at teatime. This was unless we came home early with injuries that needed stitching at the hospital from the daily stone fights with rival gangs. A common sight in our area of town was a gang of lads going past with one of the gang howling, a stream of blood flowing down his head, making their way towards North Lonsdale hospital for stitching. One or two youths lost an eye then everyone would stop throwing stones for a while. There cannot be many young lads who did not have festering knees from wearing short trousers while climbing trees and cliffs. Both my knees are heavily scarred to this day.

Most families had a radio usually Redifusion in the house before television became affordable. At night we would all listen to Jimmy Clitheroe, Billy Cotton and later on Radio Luxembourg.

A new family move into the other end of our street but we could not get on with their two boys. One day we were having a stone fight with them and they ran out of stones to throw back at us. The oldest boy dashed into his backyard coming out with fist size lumps of coal to throw at us. The adrenalin was flowing, we were suffering several hits from their accurate aim, our gang would all have bruises from this battle we were losing. Reluctantly I ran into my backyard bringing out some handy sized pieces of coal to throw back, thinking that if dad sees me I will regret it. To this day I can still recall clearly what happened next. Throwing my lump of coal towards the oldest boy it had the perfect trajectory sailing high into the sky in a graceful curve, then falling accurately right onto his forehead as he looked up in horror. I was willing him to throw himself to one side like you were supposed to do. Dramatically the coal shattered on impact blood spurt out like a fountain from his head. We were all shocked, then the boy let out an unearthly scream, his mother ran out and hustled him into the house.

This we knew was really serious and would involve a trip to hospital for the poor boy. My so called friends had all run to tell the lad's mother that it was me who was the cause of her poor boys misery not them! Knowing that retribution would be sought by the injured party made me look for a suitable hiding place. I needed to find sanctuary very quickly.

It would be safe to say that I was petrified of my father's wrath when he found out what I had done, not forgetting the waste of valuable coal. Starting to panic I spotted the upturned two wheeled barrow in our backyard, nipping inside it thinking it was a stupid place to hide assuming that my discovery would be very soon.

Two hours later I was still in the upturned wooden barrow getting cramp, feeling the world was against me. When I saw through a crack in the barrow's floor boards the lad, plus his very angry mother entering our backyard. On his head was an enormous white bandage that looked like an Indian turban, somehow I knew they were going to milk this opportunity to have me well and truly punished. Blimey the lad was still bloody crying after all this time he had no chance of ever getting into my gang, the cry baby. When dad heard her out, he said effectively that he was going to beat the crap out of me when I eventually turned up, but that in the mean time I had disappeared. My so called mates enthusiastically joined in the witch hunt for me, an action disloyal in my opinion that would be addressed by me later. It became dark I was scared and very hungry, frankly amazed that nobody had found me in such an obvious hiding place. Time to face the music I knew this was only delaying the inevitable punishment. There was even talk of the police being called in at this point. It would be safe to say my father was a bad tempered man he did not hold back with the leather belt, me not crying only made him worse. I did wrong, received my punishment that was the way of the world.

When on our way to Walney Island to pick winkles, we had to pass rows of lovely houses each with a lovely front garden. I used to stare at these houses wondering if it was possible that one day maybe I could have enough money to own one. It was difficult to imagine actually owning a garden and having our own bathroom. The contrast between where I lived and this nice area made it seem just a pipedream.

CHAPTER TWO

One of the next street's gang was killed when a tunnel in the sand cliffs at Rampside collapsed on him. This happened the day after we had dug a similar cave in the same place it was a tragic accident which upset all our community.

I was with my brothers chasing each other home from Barrow Park one morning. My accident prone brother somehow managed to slash his knee on a nail. We were horrified to see blood pouring from the loose skin flapping up and down has he walked. A knee sock was hastily wrapped around the knee we escorted him home screaming in shock and pain. He must have lost a lot of blood looking behind at the trail he was leaving. This was the same brother who had the next even worse accident! Our gang had a stupid dare we used to walk along the high brick parapet wall on Greengate Street Bridge which crossed over the main railway lines into Barrow train station. My dads tarmac plant was alongside the railway lines, we would walk across from one side of the bridge to the other showing off at how brave we were. Lucky for me this day when I lost my balance I fell inwards onto the pavement, unlucky for my brother he fell outwards off the bridge, falling from a great height onto the railway lines. Poor lad ended up in intensive care in our usual hospital, the lucky part was a steam train did not run over him. This put an end to this particular dare.

The hospital authorities reported mum to social services due to the many incidents happening. They threatened to put us all into care if it happened again. It didn't help that we had got to know the names of all the nursing staff! My eldest sister ended up in care, going away from home for many years. Poor mum we must have been a handful for her to put up with.

Watching a film at the Ritz cinema one day starring Hayley Mills in 'Pollyanna' it showed an idyllic family, the mother always came to their bedroom to give them a goodnight kiss. That night I called my mother up stairs to ask her for a goodnight kiss, she looked at me strangely saying "I worry about you sometimes Norm" promptly left leaving me with a red face and still no kiss! Thinking about this over the years I never saw my parents ever kiss, hug each other or us ever.

My one pair of trousers had patches on patches, tree and rock climbing knocked hell out of clothes nearly every boy had festering scabby knees. I never had hand me downs from my brothers because they wore out their clothes completely and afterwards being only fit for rags. There used to be a small scrap yard with a place to take your rags in the back street off Greengate Street hill. Woollens would be weighed perhaps a few coppers given. Several rag and bone men would be sat around a brazier, roasting potatoes, warming their hands, the smell in that yard made us gag. We used to ask our neighbours if they had any woollens or pop bottles we could take back to the corner shop for the refund to pay for our Saturday morning trip to the Ritz cinema. All the kids loved Jimmy the man who worked there for years he would shine his torch on us threatening to evict us for misbehaving. If there were six of us two would pay to go in and open the emergency exit doors to let the other four in, we would get away with this trick most times if caught all got a clip around the ears. Flash Gordon, The Lone Ranger, Three Stooges, Old Mother Riley and all the cartoons were very popular we soon preferred the colour films to the black and white.

Weekends dad spent any spare money on beer in his favourite working men's clubs drinking his self stupid, we used to see him staggering along Rawlinson Street, sometimes on all fours minus his hat and coat singing away not a care in the world. My mates and I would gather around him, helping him home before he was arrested. Mind you he received a right ear bashing from tee total mother. She would tell me to take a bucket up to his bedroom I was amazed how in the morning it was full to the brim. Great care was needed not to spill any of the pee on the way to the back yard toilet being so heavy I had to use two hands to carry it, the smell being vile. Drunk, dad could be very nasty often threatening to leave us all, saying he was sick of us, but in time we realised it was just the beer talking. Once or twice I would be woken up at two in the morning by dad carrying mums big trifle that he had taken out of the fridge holding it right under my nose, then shoving a spoon in my hand telling me to eat it.

He was drunk as a skunk belting me when I refused, other times I woke up to see him peeing in the corner of my bedroom against the wall. When you are only young it is a bit scary, we were all frightened of him and his bad temper. He came back from the club on Sunday afternoon drunk carrying a bundle of last week's comics bought at half price from the newsagents. Then would bundle mum and me into his Ford Consul car, my siblings had made themselves scarce. His mate had sold the car to him cheaply being paid so much a week for it. Speeding down to the coast road on the wrong side of the road was a common occurrence nearly having us all killed! Mum had made a flask of tea and some sandwiches we would spend a happy hour reading in the car until it was time to dice with death, returning home with our fingers crossed. The inevitable happened, he was fined and banned from driving after hitting a row of parked cars coming home from his club drunk one Sunday afternoon, that put an end to mum's day out and mine thank God!

My mother loved cats even strays, several were always hanging around our back door knowing she was a soft touch. Home from school this particular evening mum was feeding the cats from a tin of salmon, on the table was our meal a big plate of jam sandwiches! One night I was kept awake by strange noises which seemed to be coming from under the bed. In the morning when it was light I peeked under our bed and saw mum's cat with nine new born kittens, she had made a cosy bed using my only pair of trousers. After giving mother cat a stroke then a tickle I admired her kittens wishing that we could keep them all. My first thought was I am going to smell even worse at school today, next was how happy the mother cat was purring away, talk about the cat that got the cream! Looking around I found a small cardboard box and transferred the kittens into it so I could retrieve my trousers, a wet flannel cleaned off most of the goo, then off I went to school still sporting some colourful stains!

All through my lessons I fretted about the kittens knowing what dad was going to do when he came in from work. That evening he told me to fetch a bucket full of water and a heavy slate. I begged him to let me take them to the RSPCA but he would not listen to me. Pushing me out of his way he put the kittens into the bucket placing the slate over the top. I was crying, mums cat was howling. When it was all still in the bucket he flushed them all down the toilet, it was a long time before I could get this out of my mind having recurring nightmares over the next few years about it. I never forgave dad it was not the first time he did it nor the last. Possibly him working on farms killing animals hardened him to it. Another upsetting thing for me was walking passed the slaughter house on the way to Thomson's brewery to give my youngest sister her sandwiches which she always forgot to take (she worked in the bottling plant for a few years). The sounds of sheep and cattle in their pens and the awful smells made me feel sick.

Abbey Road public baths was a great place to learn to swim, if we had any money left buy a cup of soup in the café afterwards to warm us up. My sister Jean received trophy's and medal's for competition swimming but due to our parent's indifference and lack of money did not pursue her talent any further. My brothers were very good football players and I even played for Barrow Boy's rugby always the position of hooker. Our team reached the inter town championship final played before a large crowd at Craven Park before the main match. We won and I would have loved to see my parent's watching me play, afterwards collecting our winners medals. All the many boats I owned over the years dad never wanted to see them, when I asked him to come down to see my new boat he told me to bring him a photograph. Mum did come down to have a trip or two on the boat when she retired so I suppose that was something. We learned to swim in junior school having one lesson a week, having to scrub our feet in a shallow bath closely scrutinised by the attendant. The water always seemed to be so bloody cold until your body got used to it. The old type swimming costumes used to sag in the water like a misshapen nappy, diving in you could surface to find your swimming trunks floating away. Learning how to swim was a skill that came in useful several times over the years saving my life on a few occasions and a friend also.

Coming home from school I found two little kittens in our back street, they took an instant shine to me following me back home. They were striped like tigers, grey fur and utterly adorable, I wanted to keep them until somebody claimed them. Finding a cardboard box I put a warm wool cardigan in for their bed, hoping my sisters would not miss it from their bedroom. The kittens were obviously very hungry so I needed to get some food quick. My friend at the top of our street fetched me a tin of cat food pinched from his mother she only had one child so was richer than us. Her three cats lived a good well fed life so my kittens were going to be subsidised if I played my cards right! The kittens were named Christopher and Columbus one had slightly different marking from the other. I kept them in the outside coalhouse and over the coming weeks trained them every day. Dad thought they belonged to a neighbour so dare not drown them. They were the cleverest kittens, teaching them to come to me when I whistled, sit and stay. They were both old enough now to walk along the backyard walls and meet other cats. The kids in our street were very impressed when they both came running whenever they heard my whistle. Both cats were waiting to greet me at home time after school every day and I had managed to feed them well enough. One day they both never came back, even mum was upset she had grown attached to my beautiful cats. Mum said they were both so clever that somebody enticed them to live with them by feeding them on tuna and salmon. For weeks afterwards I roamed around all the nearby streets looking and asking everyone if they had seen my cats, they seemed to have just vanished. We sure missed them though!

CHAPTER THREE

Being the youngest I had to run all the errands and this annoyed me thinking I would rather have taken turns with my brothers. I found it stressful because mum could not ever manage to budget the house keeping dad gave her each week. She had a slate going in every corner shop in our area, never once paying each one up to date each week. This was confusing to say the least she did not seem to care about how much was adding up each week. Mum was just happy that when I passed over her list to the shop keeper the goods were passed over the counter. It was so embarrassing for me to ask for everything on the list to be put on mum's slate all the time. Once a day was bad enough but it was up to ten times. I said "think carefully mum I am not going back again tonight" sure as eggs are eggs thirty minutes later out would come another list for me. I envied the other kids whose mums gave them money to run errands with the cash to pay the shop keeper. Very often he would lean over the counter and whisper "Ask your mum to come into the shop Norman I want a word with her!" She would just laugh and say "He was lucky to have her trade and she might take her trade somewhere else if he did not change his attitude" If only he knew how many shops mum was running a slate with.

One night I blew my top after being sent four times in an hour, each time I passed the list over the counter the shop had been full. I found it so embarrassing so told her to fuck off! This was the first and last time I ever swore at her in her ninety three years of life. I woke up some time later with a bad head ache plus a ringing in both ears. Dad had heard me and laid me out with a punch to my head. I still had to go and run the errand but this time Asprin needed to be added to the list. When having money of my own later on I went round all the corner shops mum owed money paying them all off, even giving her money to start afresh. Of course this did not last she reverted back to her old ways, but at least I tried! Electricity, water, gas and any other final demands were put in a pile behind the clock on the mantel piece, to be ignored then forgotten about. Dad turned off his hearing aid, rolled another fag he had long ago given up on her.

When I was given the choice of secondary schools I picked the one furthest from where all my siblings had been, figuring the teachers there would have had a bellyful of the Pascoe name by now. My school choice was across town and consisted of a mixed class, money was still tight so my school uniform was a bit random. My trousers had a bloody big patch on the bum what a way to get noticed on your first day. The obvious nickname given at this new school was "patchy arse," I used to brood about getting my own back on these well dressed lucky bugger's that were having so much fun from my misfortune. Out of our class only a couple were in the same situation as me, the girls all looked very pretty.

I really felt out of place, most of the girls had shiny highly polished shoes that you could see your face in them. Their shirts were pristine white wore lovely blue pleated skirts, school tie even. They had full length blue coats even a leather satchel for their school books. Bloody hell these kids are well looked after I thought how come I look like my clothes have been nicked off a scarecrow! The first couple of days were all right, but the third morning in assembly a big well built lad was stood behind me, I heard him sniggering with his cronies during the first hymn. I felt his finger forcing its way into the side of my patch and into the crack of my bum. Mum had not made a great job of the stitching as usual. I heard the girls behind giggling and felt myself going bright red with embarrassment. Swinging around I smacked him between his eyes and before I could hit him again two teachers frog marched us out to the head masters study, leaving assembly in an uproar. When I explained what happened and why to our head master he could not have been more understanding. He even asked the domestic science teacher to sow the patch on properly, while I sat with a blanket over me not being in possession of any underpants. The other boy got detention. The only good thing to come out of this was nobody dared bully me again when they saw the state of the bullies face.

One weekend our gang decided to play on the old wooden jetties that jutted out into the docks. They extended about forty feet from the edge of the dock. This day we had an extra lad with us, his family was even poorer than us. He was a big strong looking boy but a bit simple and had just moved into our street, his mother asked us to take him out and befriend him. All went well until he decided to impress us by climbing up to the very top along the wooden beams high above the water. This was something none of us had the balls to do. Then he started to become cocky calling us yellow bellies, making a big mistake! We started throwing stones at him to try and scare him. Unfortunately the rock I threw hit him smack between his eyes causing him to fall headfirst into the dock (later on in life I was not a bad darter throwing all those stones was good practice!) A huge splash, then he shot to the surface coughing and spluttering, he kept going back under the water then began thrashing his arms about. Then shouting that he could not swim! One of the kids looked at me saying "You have caused it, do something"!

We crawled along the bottom beam towards him but still could not reach him he had drifted out a few yards with his thrashing about. He was going under for longer now. Thinking sod it, I jumped in and swam out to him grabbing hold of his long hair. By this time he was panicking, grabbing hold and dragging me down with him. Eventually he tired enabling me to finally get him alongside the jetty where my mates could take over. He sat on the dockside shivering with blood was running down his face. The lads had a roaring blaze going by setting fire to a small gorse bush and some driftwood managing to dry our clothes a little. Poor lad he did not say a word for the rest of the afternoon, he was in shock I think. It was hard to think of ways to avoid a good hiding from our parents after this fiasco. Our new friend was still in a daze, bleeding from his cut, it looked like two black eyes were forming already. Mind you my face had a few cuts, bruises and scratches from when he was trying to drag me down with him. My dad would not be surprised at my damage to my face I was always fighting! We left him at his backyard door and all evening I was waiting for his dad to come raging to our house, I was nervous as a turkey at Christmas. Dad was becoming a little suspicious I kept bringing him cups of tea and passing him his favourite pipe to smoke. That is how worried I was even asking mum if she wanted anything from the corner shop!

After a long sleepless night, I ate my porridge the next morning beginning to hope that I may have got away without punishment. A loud banging on the front door startled us all. Dad was stood at the kitchen sink having a shave "Who the bloody hell is that at this time of the morning" he said. My knees started to tremble with fear I started sweating and needed to wee. Mum opened the door, the lad's mother ran towards me, I flung myself backwards thinking she was going to attack me. She threw her arms around my neck and started to rain kisses on me. "Thank you, thank you" she kept saying over and over again. I could not understand what was happening after all I had nearly killed her son! "My lad finally told me what happened yesterday Norman, how you risked your life to save him after he had fallen into the docks, I shall never forget you for this!" Then one of her daughters turned up carrying a huge sponge cake and plonked it down on our table.

Me the hero! Who would have thought, the lad had not grassed me up but had come up trumps after everything, what a funny old world we live in! The cake was lovely, only spoilt by mum making me share it with all the family, that was not fair and I had to endure all those kisses! My dad said "Norm if you fell in a cess pit you would come out smelling of roses!"

My two older brothers had their own gangs having adventures completely different to us younger boys. I only saw them at night so was not close to them at all; choosing a different school from them did not help. One of my brothers could snore for England and I spent many a sleepless night tossing and turning getting more frustrated, cursing the fact that I was a very light sleeper. Kicking him only stopped the dreadful noise for short periods before he would begin to imitate a ships foghorn again. Why the rest of the family could sleep through it I will never know. One night I slept downstairs on the couch but the dreadful noise could still be heard reverberating around the house. Something in me snapped, one night I ran upstairs in a terrible temper putting one of his crusty sweaty socks in his wide open mouth. What bliss! The snoring stopped, climbing back into our bed falling into a deep contented sleep. I was rudely woken up with a jolt to find brother's hands around my throat an angry voice saying "You psycho bastard! You are dead!"

Throwing him off, I ran naked down stairs followed by a raging brother also in his birthday suit. Trapping me at the front door he proceeded to knock seven bells out of me. This only stopped when dad hollered "Stop that bloody racket or you will get my belt on your arses!" A terrible thing to be a very light sleeper!

Looking under our bed for my missing sock one morning I found a long wooden box. Dragging it from under the bed I opened it to find green bananas, packed to the brim! Suddenly I knew where they had come from. In the Evening Mail it was reported that a banana boat had come into Barrow docks to avoid a Dockers' strike at Liverpool. Somehow my brothers had managed to carry this heavy box all the way from the docks. Worst of all it looked like the greedy sods were not willing to share! It annoyed me that I was forced to share my sponge cake and it still rankled with me. I decided to eat some bananas now and hide some in the coalhouse. Over the next few days the level of bananas dropped dramatically as they were eaten before anymore could go missing. Being unripe we were all fighting to use the toilet, the diarrhoea was extremely embarrassing. In class my worst nightmare happened, I could feel the pressure building in my bowels.

Before I could say 'Fyffe's' and put my hand up to be excused, it was too late. The smell was nauseous everyone was reaching for a handkerchief to place over their nose. Our teacher dashed to open all the windows I dashed out of the classroom door heading home. There was nobody in our house so off with my trousers and a good swill in the sink to remove all the stains. My brothers informed me that they had both spent the day sitting on the toilet at school and that hell would freeze over before they would ever eat another banana!

Every spring dad would send me to a small builder's yard in School Street to fetch a bucket of lime. The builder would tell me to fill my bucket and pay him a few pennies. The lime was in a pit and I would look around for a small shovel to save using my hands. When water was added then stirred, the lime turned a lovely bright white. We would then paint our backyard walls with this lime wash, it really brightened up the yard at night on our trips to the toilet. My bucket was a heavy metal galvanised tin one, when full of lime it was bloody heavy, a struggle for me to carry all the way home. This particular day was windy and the lime pit had no shovel, the yard was empty so I filled the bucket using my bare hands. Thinking this was my lucky day the pennies saved would buy me a few sweeties made me feel like whistling! Halfway down the hill the sweat was pouring off me, and not realizing wiped my face with my hand that had been in the lime. My eyes immediately started to water because of the burning lime dust. They were both so painful that I dumped the bucket on the pavement shouting to a lady across the road that I needed to be escorted to North Lonsdale hospital straight away, my eyes felt on fire. The lovely lady took me the hundred yards to hospital quickly getting me signed in. When I told the doctor about the lime two nurses rushed me into a room and lay me on a reclining chair. Hell this must be serious I thought and asked the nurse what was going to happen next? "You could lose your eyesight you silly boy, the doctor said you have to have your eyes flushed every twenty minutes, so be patient for a few hours!" The idea that I might lose my sight upset me then I started to worry about my dad's bucket of lime abandoned on the street, what a shit day this as turned out to be. Then the idea of dad stood in our backyard holding a paint brush and his wooden stirring stick, waiting for the lime that never turned up made me laugh. Two hours later after several painful flushing of my eyes, plenty of hugs and kisses from the nurses plus chocolate biscuits. The friendly doctor announced that my left eye was back to normal but my right needed to have a bandage over it for a day or two. He gave me a telling off for playing in lime and an appointment card. Before leaving hospital I gave the nurses who were on first name terms with me a hug, they said that I looked very dashing with my white turban on! Strolling down the street all the kids were looking at me in awe thinking that my skull must have been shattered, judging by the size of the bandage. Of course my bucket was gone, (who the hell would want to steal a bucket full of lime)? Surely when dad sees the bandage he will understand? Walking down our backstreet I had a crowd of kids all excitedly asking if it was a bus that hit me. Entering our back yard, dad said "Where's my bloody bucket"

CHAPTER FOUR

Quite a few kids started shoplifting in their lunch breaks bringing stuff to school to sell. To my shame my friend and I decided to earn some money by doing the same. I thought it was the only way that I could ever have decent clothes for school, pay for school trips and not end up the only one left out. The first time I stole from Woolworths my knees were knocking, sweat was pouring off me, the adrenaline was pumping, I felt dreadful.

The amazing thing is that I was not arrested straight away. My coat had a long inside pocket ideal for concealing stolen items. The first things we stole were lipsticks and perfume that the girls at school bought eagerly. As we became bolder and better we progressed to geometry sets, pens and books, pinching to order. Most lunch times, evenings and Saturdays we visited town centre shops, supplying a growing customer base even letting the other kids pay weekly, recording payments in our note book. We were amazed how much pocket money some kids received even in those days, bearing in mind my dad had never given any of us a penny. One day I felt great going into a chippy, buying my first ever fish and chips, then sitting in the back street enjoying every scrap, savouring the novelty. With my money I bought a new school uniform plus my first underwear, strange thing was mother never noticed or ever asked where the new clothes came from. No more badly sown large patches on my backside, it felt good to blend in and possess a change of clothes like my school friends.

Paying for school trips was now no problem or sports kit, the worry of being caught shop lifting was always there. The money was being used as well to help mother pay a few urgent bills to stop us being evicted, so I felt it was just a little justified. We were never caught so I suppose we must have been good or very lucky. I remember playing in our house one day with my friends. My mother started to drag us behind the sofa to hide, pretending it was a game when the rent man came hammering on our door. This was still fresh in my mind. All my mates thought it was hilarious but I did not think it was funny to this day I have not liked owing a penny to anyone.

The area around Barrow docks was our favourite place for adventure. The best place was Wards ship breakers inside the docks, also on Ward's bank outside the dock entrance, where smaller ships were beached at high tide, then moored up for easy access. Larger ships were towed into the docks by the Cornmill sidings to be scrapped topsides first until just above the waterline, then the hull was towed out to Ward's bank by a small tug to be beached, then finished off. A steam crane pulled the cut up pieces up the banking, heaping it up ready for collection.

One Monday morning on our way to school we nicked a couple of packets of Manikin cigars from the corner shop, (we could not reach the cigarettes) then we decided to play truant heading down to the docks. To our delight a couple of old steam powered hopper barges were moored up at Ward's bank, as a bonus a steam tug was lashed alongside. The tide was full in so we had to gain access by going hand over hand up the steel mooring wires like a monkey. The work men must all have been working at the other Wards inside the dock so we had a good chance of not being spotted, the first hopper was called 'Presall Sands' the name was on the bows in big white letters. Shinning up the rusty old wires a shard went straight through my hand, the pain nearly made me leave go of the wire. I decided it was easier to carry on than to go back, the blood running down my arm was a little alarming. Climbing on board was a huge relief, and I helped my friend onto the deck, both of us panting heavily with our excursions. We stopped the bleeding with my mate's handkerchief he had thoughtfully picked off the big bits of dried snot first, it doing the trick nicely.

We explored the ship and to our delight finding she still had all the furniture in the cabins. "Blimey my mum would like all this nice furniture in Glasgow street" I said to my friend. After doing a tour of all the ships, we lit the stove in the captain's cabin and relaxed with a cigar each, both pretending that we did not feel sick. We agreed that it beat the hell out of double maths, taking an afternoon nap in the comfortable bunks, whilst waiting for the tide to fall. All too soon it was time to prepare a rope ladder to disembark, much easier than climbing back down the mooring wire. Unfortunately now the tide had left the boats, we were up to our knees in mud going ashore. My hand was still throbbing from the accident sustained when climbing aboard earlier, but we had had a great day. We had a spell of playing truant after we found a huge steam powered bucket dredger called 'Piel' moored in the Anchorline dock basin, she was waiting to be scrapped. Being coal fired these boats were uneconomical to run any longer. The dredger 'Piel' was a common sight to Barrow people chewing away the silt in Walney Channel, filling her hopper barges, thick black smoke always belching from her tall funnel. The watch man once invited me aboard one day for a mug of tea and to share his sandwiches. Seeing her laid up looking all forlorn and abandoned in a quiet corner of the docks, we sneaked aboard pinching all the old flares including the rocket gun. The cabins were all intact with furniture, the bunks still made up with pillows and blankets. All our school friends and the other gangs were impressed with our spoils, it was a wonder none of us were injured or killed when we set them all off.

Sometimes we set a bank line of fifty baited hooks off Foulney Island which was reached by a long causeway covered by the tide for several hours a day. Often the Barrow inshore lifeboat had to rescue people cut off by the tide when only halfway across. The island is a bird sanctuary with a warden who lives all summer in a caravan. This is parked at the start of the causeway in order to police it efficiently. Years ago when we camped the night waiting to fish our bank lines, we were plagued with mice and rats. There were hundreds of them stealing the nesting bird's eggs. That is why a program was started to eliminate the vermin thankfully the birds have now made a comeback. For camping Foulney was perfect for us, having masses of driftwood always washing ashore, mussel beds only a short walk away. We always caught bass on our lines and often shared the small island with expert bass anglers. For years a shelter made from driftwood stood on the very end of the island, built by the regular anglers to shelter in, we stayed one night inside when our tent blew down in a storm. The mice were actually running all over us nibbling any exposed fingers, it was the longest night we ever endured. It was pouring with rain outside and a bloody nightmare inside. We did make a nice sum of money the next morning after the storm, because along the high water mark there were several plastic current drift markers washed up. These markers were dropped into the Irish Sea to help determine the current drift along the seabed. The Fisheries Department said an award of twenty five shillings would be paid if you returned the tags with details of where they were found. Our postal orders arrived and we felt rich, beach combing paid off handsomely sometimes. There is no camping allowed on the island now, dogs have to be kept on leads in the birds breeding season, which is fair enough.

The day dad decided to sweep our chimney will stay in my mind forever. We had been sitting in a smoke filled room for a few days, when dad announced that he would sweep the soot out of the chimney the chimney sweep was a robbing bastard he reckoned. We knew dad had no money left, so if he wanted to avoid us being smoked like kippers he would have to solve this problem on his own. Dad borrowed a set of rods and a sweep's brush from a friend at work. I was designated to be his assistant for the task. An old blanket was put over the fire place with a hole cut in the centre for the rods to pass through. The top of the blanket was held in place by a row of house bricks on the mantelpiece. Dad was chuckling to himself, I heard him mutter that this job was a piece of piss, he might take sweeping up as a second job! He said to me "Did you know son on the farm I worked on, the farmer was a right miserable bastard and would not pay for a chimney sweep."

"What did he do then dad?"

"The clever bugger tied a string around his cockerel's legs, climbed onto his roof then shoved the bird down the chimney. It worked a bloody treat the flapping of the birds wings acted the same as a sweeps brush, you should have seen the pile of soot that bird bought down the chimney!"

Suddenly I had a sense of foreboding that something would go drastically wrong this day.

Dad shoved the rods up the chimney and we could hear the sound of the soot falling down behind the blanket. About halfway up the chimney the rods would not go any further up, something was blocking its progress. No matter how hard dad shoved the brush would go no further.

"Dam and bloody blast, this is not going to beat me, a loose brick must be blocking the chimney, but it will not get the better of me!"

Dad went next door to borrow a ladder.

"What are you going to do dad?"

"I will put the rods down the chimney from the roof, when you see or hear the brush hitting the fireplace grate, come outside and shout up to me, I will stop putting any more rods on."

Now I could see some possible flaws in dad's plan but did as I was told.

I could hear the brush coming down the chimney and a roar of loose soot cascading down, I could hear dad vigorously pushing the rods to dislodge the obstruction. A moment later the brush plus blanket shot out of the fireplace in a huge cloud of erupting soot cloud, hitting me in the chest propelling me across the room. Everything went black, minutes later when the air cleared I could make out mum stood in the doorway, covered in soot from head to toe holding two mugs of tea with a thick layer of fine soot on top! Except for the whites of our eyes we looked like chimney sweeps on a busy day. Mum looked around the room and for the first time ever I saw her crying. Two white streaks ran down her face where her tears flowed, she was devastated. Our cat that used to be grey was now a sooty black colour, sitting on the window sill shaking soot off her whiskers, looking a little bemused by it all!

Dad appeared in the doorway looked at the scene, pointed to me saying "This is his bloody fault mother he was supposed to warn me when he saw the brush at the bottom, he's fucking useless!"

The mess caused by the soot took a lot of hard work to clean up being so fine it had penetrated every nook and cranny in the house. The house smelled of soot for days, we could not believe how difficult it was to remove it all, before getting back to normality and order. All this grief caused by trying to save a few pounds by not hiring a proper chimney sweep.

CHAPTER FIVE

Boarding and exploring all these hulks waiting to be scrapped gave us a taste for boating. After spotting an advert in dad's Exchange & Mart for a genuine ex RAF survival inflatable dinghy, we pooled all our money, duly sending off a postal order. The next couple of weeks were spent in a state of high excitement waiting for the post to arrive at our friend's house.

Our friend's parents took in lodgers who worked at Vickers shipyard, his dad allowed us to use his coal cellar for our head quarters. My friend was the most popular boy in the school, because one of his lodgers gave him all his dirty magazines after he had finished reading them. For a small fee we hired them out to our school friends, there was always a waiting list to borrow them, we found it very lucrative. At last the big day arrived we carried the large package down the steps of the cellar the inflatable dinghy was bright yellow. This was made from very thick rubber, came supplied with wooden paddles also including a foot pump. A box with a repair kit in case of puncture was included, but no matter how much we abused the dinghy the repair kit was never used.

We agreed to use Cavendish dock which held several acres of water for our maiden voyage and needed to keep this a secret otherwise all the kids from our school would have turned up. After school we loaded up the dingy in dad's wheel barrow and went to the dock. In no time at all we had the dinghy pumped up hard. This huge dock was used to top up the rest of the dock system to keep a constant level at all times for the nuclear submarines, also as a coolant for the coal powered power station nearby. We had a great time paddling around the huge tract of water until dark pretending to be commando's preparing to land on an enemy shore, a lovely feeling coming ashore by the light of the moon. We were all knackered but happy tramping through the streets taking all our gear back to the cellar. We always took the dinghy with us when camping at weekends and were looking forward to the long summer holidays.

The summer holiday arrived and we planned to camp at Thorny Nook on Walney Island. One of our friends begged his dad to loan us his brand new tent instead of us using my leaky one. Against his dad's better judgment we got the loan of the new one. His dad said if it came back damaged we would have to suffer the consequences, so off we went with a wheel barrow full of gear on the long walk to Walney Island. The weather was lovely and sunny our posh tent was all set up, the camp fire lit the kettle boiling. We always liked to have plenty of wood so walked up and down the beach collecting driftwood, enjoying our beach combing. In those days you really did find interesting things washing up on the tide, things like trawl netting, fishing floats, wooden hatch covers washed off ships in storms, all kinds of lovely shaped coloured bottles, you were always surprised at what the nights tide bought in.

When the tide was in we paddled our dinghy in the sea, at low tide we collected winkles, cockles and mussels, if we were lucky the odd crab or lobster off the outlying scars. Being boys mostly we were good, but on the cold windy days we could not get out to sea in our dinghy we became a little bored. Somebody came up with the idea of collecting the many hairspray aerosol cans washed up on the beach, then putting them on our campfire. When they heated up, depending on how much hairspray was left in the cans, they would explode with a loud bang shooting up into the skies, leaving behind a spectacular flaming trail. This was very exciting but very dangerous, we all loved doing it. Then we found the explosive power of metal polish cans! One of our mates came running into the camp holding a half full tin of metal polish he had just found washed up on the tide. We were all very excited, anticipating the spectacular bang and fireball. We realised that it would be sensible to all stand further back from this anticipated explosion, then threw the tin into the middle of our blazing camp fire. What a bang! A huge ball of fire flew within inches of my head. I could feel the intense heat on my face. Thinking bloody hell that nearly took my head off, I turned to see the fire ball fly straight into the open tent door making the tent become an instant inferno. Sleeping bags including all our clothes were consumed in a very short time, only leaving a mound of ashes where our tent had been.

Well I nearly wet my pants, the lad whose dad owned the tent did, what a bummer the holiday was ruined. Sat around the camp fire that night thinking how odd we looked, possessing no eyebrows between us, we discussed what to do next. Our friend's dad was a bad tempered sod at the best of times, he had warned us what to expect, our prospects looked bleak. At daybreak we looked at each other's sooty faces and knew we would have to make our way home, we were all very hungry. Walking home dragging our feet across the Jubilee Bridge then the High Level bridge back to Glasgow Street nobody was saying much. At our friends door we told him what to say, patted him on his back then ran like hell. Our friend told his dad that a bolt of lightning hit the tent and set it on fire we were only saved by an act of God. This lame explanation only infuriated his dad who promptly bought out the leather belt. Hours later we met up to compare red raw buttocks, the consensus of opinion was that we had got off lightly we still had my leaky tent to use next time, so things were not all bad. We all had to sleep face down for a few nights.

Another camping site of ours was North Walney which had lovely lagoons that had been dug out for the sand and gravel extraction. This was a beautiful place to camp, but a long way from a fresh water supply. The south end at Thorny Nook was nice and grassy to pitch our tent near the cliffs whereas the north we camped in sand dunes. The area is now a special protected site and is the home of the rare Natterjack toads (they have a pretty yellow stripe running down the back). They were very popular with us because they came out at dusk making loud ratchet sounds that can be heard a mile away on a calm night. Claimed to be the noisiest amphibians in Europe we could imagine we were camping in Africa! Also it is the home of the Walney rare geranium plant, a variety of Bloody Cranesbill. We were told at school that Bronze and Iron Age pottery including flints had been found at the north tip of the island. We found the remains of their mussel and cockle discarded heaps, also small pieces of pottery which we handed in to Barrow museum.

Off the very end of Walney lies the wreck of an old collier called 'Anastasia' we could visit it at low tide excited to explore the remains. Sometimes a large shoal of mullet numbering hundreds were trapped in the pool left around the wreck, it was so easy to spear a couple to cook on our campfire. We never possessed a local tide book but using our common sense soon worked the tides out. Paddling around the old gravel lagoons in our rubber dinghy was great fun, also very safe compared to when we went to sea, there was amazing bird life all around us. I could never imagine that part of my future would involve working here digging more lagoons for a career. Or that I would live on another protected site in a remote cottage and monitor Natterjack toads for the Herpetological Society in the future. Looking back how lucky we were to have all these adventures with good friends and parents who let us enjoy using our freedom and imagination.

CHAPTER SIX

We convened a special meeting in the cellar on offer to us was a two man canoe very cheap, a big step up from our inflatable dinghy. The problem was our funds were low, especially now the shoplifting had been given up. One of the gang started an evening and Saturday job where old railway carriages were dismantled for scrap content. His task was to unscrew all the brass and copper fittings, ash trays, door handles, brass screws, even the lead acid batteries from under the carriages. My sister worked for Cahill's a family owned business selling whole sale groceries to all the corner shops in Barrow including the Lake District. She managed to get me evenings plus Saturday work putting up the orders, also loading the delivery vans. Before the arrival of the supermarkets corner shops were still very profitable. Cahill's had taken over nearly all of Whittaker Street as a warehouse, storing thousands of cases of groceries. They employed office staff, warehouse men and delivery drivers making it a very good business indeed. The place was like a maze, different rooms for cases of soup, beans, you name it they stocked it. My job was to have a list and pull a trolley around putting up shop orders. It took a while to find my way around but got there eventually. My favourite store room was for the dried fruit, every variety you could imagine packed and stored in tea chests lined with tin foil to keep fresh. Stuffing my face and pockets I lingered far too long in there getting a bollocking from the warehouse boss, when arriving home mum thought it was strange my appetite had gone. The money was good and the firm treated me well. At one time sister, brother and mother worked for Cahill's too, mum doing a bit of cleaning. All good things come to an end we had eventually saved up enough money for our canoe so packed in our jobs. My sister reported that the firm were back to making a profit with their dried fruit sales after my departure.

The canoe man was paid, it was collected along with two sets of paddles and we were back in business. My friend's dad was in his usual position by the cellar door, feet up by the roaring fire, he did not bat an eye lid when we slid this canoe passed him. Our friend's mum was kept busy looking after the lodgers so we did not see her very often. His father was a labourer in the ship yard, walked over the bridge to work each day, came home spent the evenings by the fire contented with his lot, perhaps we may have been his entertainment. Summer holidays were here again so the wheel barrow and our home made canoe carrier made from pram wheels were all loaded up, then we headed for Walney Island.

Our tent was erected, the camp fire lit, loads of driftwood collected from the high tide mark. We were all excited about the forth coming adventures we were going to have. It was good to be away from our parents and adult supervision. The days flew by we were enjoying every moment, the weather was very good. When the food supplies were dwindling we collected cockles and mussels, boiling them up over our camp fire. We dug up lugworms for bait, laying out a bank line with thirty hooks which caught enough flounders and bass to feed us.

When our money ran out we climbed over the back wall of the nearest pub stealing some empty pop bottles to return later for a refund. Of course over doing it resulting in the landlord giving us all a good clip around our ears for our cheek! The sun was shining we had managed to not burn our tent down this year so everything was just fine. Each day the sea was calm we went out in our canoe at high tide looking seawards at the large fleet of trawlers working just off the rough ground. Towing their nets up and down day and night taking advantage of the good weather.

The sea was flat calm and one little trawler was very near to the shore.

The temptation was too much, we decided to paddle our canoe out to them, the little fishing smack had a small leg o' mutton sail on the boom which I learned later was used as a steadying sail. The boat was a famous class of fishing boat called a 'Morecambe Bay' prawner or half decker, built many years ago to fish in our local waters. The name painted on her bow was too faded to read, I thought she sat in the water like a duck!

Two men in black oilskins were on board, one man was on the long tiller steering her, two rope warps led over the stern I knew they were slowly pulling a trawl net behind the boat.

Little did I know then what an effect it would have on me that day meeting these fishermen from Fleetwood, that one day I would be the proud owner of two of these fine vessels, having the privilege to fish one of these fine historical boats full time. We were both shattered after paddling so far out to sea, my back as usual was giving me grief. Lucky for us we saw the smack stop towing, then begin to pull in their trawl net. One man walked to the bow of the boat to start the capstan winch to commence pulling in both trawl warps, coiling the wet rope in a circle neatly on the foredeck. The men did not speak but went about their work in silence. Next the two otter boards (which spread the mouth of the net) broke the surface and were quickly lifted aboard. The bright orange trawl came to the surface then was pulled aboard, leaving the heavy cod end full of glistening fish lying alongside the boat. A heavy hook was put into a rope strop placed around the net. The cod end (where the fish collected) was then lifted up and emptied into a fish pound. Onto the side deck a mass of sea life spilled out, such a variety I had never imagined. Huge plaice with big red spots flapping about the deck, cod with big bulging eyes, a huge skate with barbed tail holding a whiting in its jaws, brown crabs and a big blue lobster.

We held onto the side of the boat enthralled at what was in the fish pound, what bright colours we saw, sea anemones, many starfish, whelks, clams and stones with kelp still attached. Many sea gulls appeared wheeling and diving for any tiny fish that fell out of the net, the noise was deafening as the gulls fought over scraps. We were exited thinking we might be given some fish to take back with us.

Only when the fishermen had stowed away the gear ready for their next tow did the skipper speak to us. "You fucking pair of idiots, what the fucking hell possessed you to paddle this far out? Where are your parents they want fucking locking up, you have not even got life jackets on!" After that ranting and raging his voice softened, they helped us to get aboard the trawler then lifted our canoe onto the deck. A huge mug of sweet tea and a jam butty was placed in our hands, "Look boys sorry to have shouted at you and used bad language but you have put yourselves in great danger, we are going to take you into the beach where you set off from, making sure you get back ashore safely" He explained to me about spring tides and the fact that the tide had turned making it impossible to paddle against it, we would have been washed out to sea if they had not been there, a valuable lesson to learn.

True to his word he steamed the smack towards the beach at 'Thorny Nook,' only when the smacks keel hit the bottom did he put the canoe over the side seeing us safely into it. A large bag of fish was dropped into our canoe they also made us promise to never repeat a daft trick like that again. They gave us a cheerful wave as the smack steamed back out to sea. The deck hand started to gut the fish, the huge flock of sea gulls started following the boat seawards, fighting over the discarded fish guts.

Our friends left behind on the beach were green with envy when they saw this small fishing smack bringing us right into the beach, when they saw the bag of large fish we had been given could not believe our luck. We all carried the canoe up the beach I filleted our fish for dinner telling the lads all about our adventure over and over again! Meeting the fishermen made me obsessed about owning my own little fishing boat and making trawling my career.

When back at school we had a great tale to tell our school mates and teachers, even though they all gave the impression that we had been telling lies. Looking back it was strange me picking a fishing career, in our town it was expected that you became an apprentice in Vickers or one of the many other trades in Barrow. My father thought that I was mad, he firmly advised me to get a trade, saying that Barrow was not even a fishing port, the part timers were only playing at fishing, not even going past the end of Walney Island!

CHAPTER SEVEN

After the camping holiday was over we all agreed a bigger boat was required, so arranged a meeting down the cellar, only three members were left in our gang now. We asked our friend's dad if he would like a mug of tea, then asked him if he would agree to sign the hire purchase agreement for a brand new plywood dinghy plus 'Seagull' outboard motor from Dolings shop in Dalton road. The next week saw us at Dolings and his dad signing the papers, outside the shop he gave us the weekly paying in book then walked off! What a fine man, was he mad or a saint, we repaid his trust in us by never missing a payment. The lovely varnished dinghy plus the outboard motor were delivered to Ferry beach along with oars, a new anchor, no life jackets though we could not afford any, also our gang was down to two now.

The only full time inshore fisherman who was based at Ferry beach helped us put our new boat on a safe mooring. He took the time to help two daft but keen boys to try not to drown ourselves. The heavy outboard motor and oars we carried home each time we sailed out for a fishing trip, making it hard work, until another kind boat club member gave us a key to his shed. I returned to my old job at Cahill's, thanks to my sister, promising to leave the dried fruit alone this time. My friend went back to his old job dismantling old railway carriages.

Slowly we managed with several dangerous moments to become good at rowing in the vicious tide races in Walney channel where the rise and fall of tide can be over thirty feet. We had to learn how to use the eddy and slack water periods to your advantage. In the event of losing an oar would see you being swilled out of the north end of Walney channel then out to sea! How we avoided drowning ourselves I will never know, somebody was up there looking after us. Nobody wore life jackets then because they were still bulky, there were plenty stowed inside cabins for emergency. Most had been board of trade style brought off liners and other various ships scrapped at Wards ship breakers. We dug bait and gained experience hand lining off Walney Island, catching codling and plaice going out with the tide coming back on the flood to save fuel, learning a little more sea sense each trip.

A lovely old fisherman showed us how to rig a hand line properly it was exciting to feel the thrill of a large fish tugging at the line wrapped around your finger. Then to give a sharp tug and realise you had actually caught a large plaice or cod was a never to be forgotten experience. I actually witnessed this man using a hand line (he called this method of fishing Kebbing) pulling a large lobster up near the Vickers slipway. The lobster would not let go of the bait and he gently eased it into his rowing boat without scaring it into letting go. Now that was skill, this old man had retired and owned a large, very heavy wooden dinghy. Most days he fished a few yards away in the middle of the channel always catching a feed of fish, a typical catch would be a couple of small codling, eels, a nice plaice and occasional lobster. At weekends he would drift in the centre of the channel holding up his boats bow rope asking for a tow down the channel from any boat leaving on the ebb tide, to fish all day getting a tow back on the flood. He would have a box full of prime fish that did not cost him a penny in fuel cost.

One Friday afternoon in spring four of us jigged school, loaded our dinghy with tent and food then sailed down to Piel Island to camp near the ruins of the castle. The monks of Furness abbey had built this in the 12th century to house their bales of sheep wool, until sailing ships came to pick it up. We all had heard tales of monks haunting the ruins so kept away from the castle when it was dark. We pulled the dinghy above the high water mark and pitched the tent. It was still daylight for a while so I decided to collect some whelks for our supper in nearby Bass pool. Nobody fancied coming with me, so with the only pair of outsize waders that we shared between us and a bucket I set off. Muttering to myself, thinking how lazy my friend's were. At first it was easy walking over the mussel beds towards the middle of the pool, finding a few nice size whelks in the gulley bottoms. The curlews were calling I thought how peaceful it was and what a contrast to the grim backstreets back home in

Barrow. It was certainly a warm pleasant evening. The next gulley I came to was quite deep, and when standing at the bottom was out of sight of anyone ashore.

Suddenly the sand was quivering like jelly I could feel my legs going deeper into the sand, until it was soon up to my knees. Trying to lift my legs was like trying to pull them out of treacle the more I struggled the deeper my legs sank. I thought what a stupid way to die, time was against me, the tide was starting to flood in and I was losing valuable time needed to get to the safety of the shore. By my stupidity in coming out on my own I was in danger of drowning before any help could arrive. Forcing myself to stay calm, not to panic, I realised that my waders were indeed stuck here forever, but my feet could still pull out if I left the waders. Pulling out one foot then the other, flopping full length onto the mud to spread my weight evenly, I started to move lizard like towards the top of the gulley. The sand getting firmer the higher I went. Looking back down into the gulley to see the flood tide spreading around my stuck waders made me realise how lucky I had been and so near death. If my waders had not been several sizes too big for me, I would still be stuck firmly in the sinking sand of the gulley bottom and certain death. Quickly making my way back to the safety of Piel Island to stay ahead of the incoming tide, I collapsed onto the grass my body shaking with fright, realising how close the grim reaper had come to claiming me. Putting myself in danger all for a bucket of whelks, which were still there in the bottom of that gulley, adjoining the pair of waders.

Writing about my terrible experience in Bass pool all those years ago I noticed that it had just made headlines in our local news paper. A similar situation recently happened to a man who also got trapped there. He was only just rescued in time by using his mobile phone to call for help. Fortunately he was also saved before the tide flooded in. That poor man must have been scared out of his wits, I certainly was! When I walked into our tent that night covered head to toe in thick mud and still shaking, one of the lads quipped "I suppose whelks are off the menu tonight Norm?"

We behaved ourselves at the boat club gradually becoming accepted by the other boatmen. Some were great characters and always had interesting stories to tell, we even were invited to crew on their early morning fishing trips. We were up at four in the morning grabbing a few jam sandwiches then a quick dash down to Ferry beach hoping the boat had not left without us. Our parents had no idea what we were up to they were used to us always being out of the house. The skipper usually made us row him aboard, while he primed the petrol / paraffin engine and started to swing the starting handle. We stood on the bow ready to drop off the mooring at his command feeling very important. Then off down the channel, the skipper put me on the tiller whilst he checked his net for rips or holes, the rats would often eat through the trawl meshes to get at any old fish left in the net by a lazy crew not cleaning up properly. My mate would be in the cabin brewing up, if we were lucky the skipper would have bought some bacon with him. Some days there would be fifteen or twenty boats all steaming down channel heading for different fishing grounds. The skippers calling out friendly insults to each other, one lovely converted lifeboat called the 'Crack o' Noon' getting stick because he unusually made an early start for once!

One early summer morning most of the Barrow weekend fishing boats headed down channel at the same time on the ebb tide in a heavy mist. Half an hour later it was so thick you could not even see a man stood on the bow of the boat. Instead of dropping our anchors we all carried on like the blind leading the blind. We ran aground becoming well and truly stuck on a sandbank, we cursed our luck. The skipper even made us jump overboard in waist deep freezing water in an effort to push the boat back into deeper water. Our day was completely wasted so we sat in the cockpit in foul moods wet up to our waists, waiting for the tide to leave us and the fog to lift. The morning sun burnt off the fog revealing boats ebbed out all the way down the channel, everyone climbing overboard carrying deck brushes to spend the enforced time scrubbing the weed off the hull bottoms! The lucky few that managed to stay in deep water carried on with their days trawling, lucky devils!

The only inshore full time fisherman at Barrow was a character called Cecil Nicholas, he lived in Earl Street only a short walk to Ferry Beach where he had a hut and owned two fishing boats. The largest was a thirty foot ex ship's lifeboat called 'Star of Hope' she was clinker built. The smaller built by him in his shed over the winter months was called 'Daisy' she was built on the lines of a shrimper being carvel built. He was Cec or Nicky to his friends and was never heard to swear no matter the provocation, he served with distinction in the war. One day he showed me a medal awarded to him for staying at his post while under attack manning a Bofors gun. The first time I ever saw trammel netting was the time Nicky took me down the Walney channel on the 'Star of Hope' towing his heavy wooden dinghy behind us loaded with two hundred yards of heavy trammel net. Also crewing that day was his best friend Jimmy who was the first man kind enough to give us a key to his boat shed to store our gear.

Trammel nets are set a little before low water because if too much tide is running they can be plastered with weed or jelly fish and will not fish. They are set across the channel, anchored at each end marked by buoys usually with a flag on top. The top headline floats with a row of corks along the length of it and the bottom of the net is weighted by lead weights at regular intervals, creating a long net that stands upright in the tide. The net consist of three layers, a small 40mm mesh rising to 40cc and when a fish pushes into this it forms a pocket in which the fish becomes trapped. These trammels are very heavy and take some cleaning afterwards, they catch all the debris floating in the water if the tide starts running and it can take days to clean them out, in those days lots of sewers emptied into the channel bringing all sorts of horrible things like used condoms and sanitary wear. In summer swarms of jellyfish swim over or through the nets ripping off their tentacles which cause stings similar to nettle stings. When shaking fish out of the nets your face gets stung countless times with the residue of these jelly fish and is very unpleasant. There is a tale to tell about these jellyfish later on in my story.

On the occasions that they were very badly fouled you had to bring them ashore hanging the net on hooks along a wall spending many laborious hours cleaning. That is why they have been superseded by very light monofilament netting which is set by the 1000 yards by modern fishermen calling them Gill nets.

When we reached our fishing place which was off Roa Island lifeboat station, I rowed the heavy wooden dinghy across the width of the channel in a straight line where Nicky indicated, the first anchor was thrown shore wards in one foot of water and as I rowed Jimmy paid out the net over a canvas cover draped over the dinghy transom so it would not snag. The place we fished through was called Cope's Hole and the net sank to the seabed thirty feet under us then gradually the net corks appeared when I rowed into shallow water on the other side of the channel. When we came to the last of the net I threw out the anchor and marker buoy, I was shattered. "That was hard graft Jimmy" I said. "That's nothing Norm you have not finished yet!" I rowed us over to where Nicky was waiting for us in the 'Star of Hope' and tied astern. Nicky explained to me what happens next, now it was dead low water. He handed me a posser (used in dolly tubs to agitate the water), it was copper with a row of holes around it attached to a heavy wooden pole. I gathered that Nicky was steaming a few hundred yards up tide towing me behind him and every few yards I had to vigorously plunge the posser hard into the water to create noise to scare the dormant fish towards our trammel net. We would zig zag across the channel gradually getting to our net, also Nicky chucked overboard a length of rope plus chain to drag behind the big boat to stir the fish up. I later did this for the skipper of the 'Sea King' and he swore by towing a heavy brass ship's bell behind us saying it was his secret weapon! Never have I experienced the work involved using a posser, you gradually develop a routine, sweat pours out of you no matter how cold the day is, to slack off slightly for a breather brings down the wrath of the skipper. At first you are annoyed at getting soaked off the splashes then are grateful for the cooling down effect, by the time the skipper has reached his net you gratefully put the posser down and swear to not do it again.

The best part of course is picking the net up to see what success you may have, maybe a feast or a famine, before the tide gets too strong. You guessed right, it was me doing the rowing whilst Jimmy picked the marker buoy and the first anchor up. Jimmy started to pull the net over the transom of our dinghy laying it down as evenly has he could, no fish for the first twenty yards, then white shapes could be seen under the water. Soon I saw that they were large flounders, white bellies and brown tops. Then a large gap with nothing in until we came to the net picked up in the deepest part of the channel, containing codling after codling, dozens and dozens fresh alive, flapping and gasping in their death throes. This was amazing catching so many meant that you could not spend time picking them out of the meshes, which would have to wait until we picked all the net up. Then we rowed alongside the Star of Hope which had been anchored in the channel edge. The last ten yards of net were plastered with yet more flounders, now we had a huge heap of net plus fish weighing down our dinghy, with lots of sea water slopping about in the bilges making it hard to row. We tied fore and aft alongside Nikky then started to pull the net aboard disentangling the meshed fish as we came to them, filling up boxes and relaying the net neatly ready for using again. Nikky seemed surprised at the amount of fish we had caught and asked me to pick up the anchor. We were heading home on the flood tide to Barrow, needing to be ready for Vickers workers coming down to Ferry Beach at lunch time to pick up their orders.

We took all the fish ashore, Nikky put an old zinc bath full of flounders another full of codling in the shed doorway. Giving me a small blackboard with fresh fish chalked on it told me to carry it to the lane entrance of Ferry Beach. He stood at his bench filleting for the customers that preferred their fish that way and showed me how to use a filleting knife properly, which I found extremely useful in later years when I owned a fishmongers shop. Somebody saved newspapers for him to wrap up their fish to avoid the slime getting onto their clothes.

Nikky must have got fed up with me but was too good mannered to say that I was a nuisance. Several times a day I would go to his boat shed asking for various nuts, bolts, washers, lengths of copper pipe, you name it I asked him for it. I used to lay my boat up for repairs just along from his shed so it was very convenient for me and saved leg work. His shed had everything imaginable stowed away in various tins and jars hidden in cupboards, also down below his floor boards. Lengths of timber were stowed in his rafters and below in his cellar. All stuff donated over the years from friends that worked in Vickers to help him keep his two fishing boats in commission. When I asked for something awkward for him to find or if he was very busy he would 'Tut Tut' saying people think this is a yacht chandlers not a blooming boat shed! To his credit he never once refused me anything but I did notice if he did not like somebody he always said to them that he had nothing they asked for, and to try another shed! When Nikky passed away I helped to clear out his shed it took a long time to remove all the boat treasures accumulated over his lifetime.

On a post outside the shed window 'Snowy' the one legged seagull called out to him for his daily feed of fish bits. This must have been the luckiest seagull in England having been fed daily by Nikky since he was newly hatched. Snowy never had to hunt for food ever in his life. After Nikky passed away I knew that he would have wished for Snowy to be looked after. I managed to do it with the help of some of the boating lads. Snowy was so frail latterly that he just hopped about on his one leg not being able to fly anymore. His demise came not from old age, but from a bad tempered car driver who ran over him not having the patience to let him get out of the way quickly enough. Needless to say this man was very unpopular with some of us! Nikky was one of life's gentlemen, a great character living his dream down Ferry beach. His needs were simple, with his circle of loyal customer's calling each day at the shed door for their bag of fish. He did not have to sail far the channel had ample fish to sustain his needs on his own doorstep. When I became a full time fisherman we had to roam further afield all over the Irish Sea in our quest to fill up our boat with fish, in order to keep three or four men in wages.

Most boats in Walney channel were converted ships life boats bought from Wards ship breakers for only one pound a foot, the usual length of boat being thirty feet. Several types and sizes were bought off the various ships broken up over the years including huge ocean liners, cargo ships, dredgers, warships, even submarines. All kinds of marine gear could be purchased, from ship's wheels, compasses, anchor, chain, teak or mahogany cabin furniture, if you had the cash just about anything.

We trawled the ebb tide and low water pulling the trawl in by hand, one of us on each warp finding it very hard work, also to keep your balance on the deck was not very easy, I nearly went overboard on several occasions with the boat rolling her side decks under. What excitement when the cod end was emptied on the deck to see the array of fish and other sea life flapping about fresh alive! This thrill never ever left making me even more determined to become a full time fisherman. When the flood tide started the trawl gear was packed neatly away, the skipper steamed for home, leaving us to gut the baskets of fish, swilling the deck down with sea water using a bucket with rope attached to the handle.

The engine was put on full power to get the skipper back to Barrow to sell his catch in his favourite pub and we proudly walked home with our feed of fish. We were always taught to leave the boat as we found it, all washed down, every fish and little crab removed from the net, all pieces of seaweed removed, wheelhouse windows washed with fresh water. Only when the skipper was happy you all jumped into the dinghy with the days catch to row ashore. In those days five gutted plaice were tied together with a strong steel wire and sold as a 'string' of fish for half a crown. The change to using plastic bags to sell the fish in was still a long time off. The fish were expertly filleted by mum, any leftover I sold to the neighbours for our new boat fund, mum was happy to keep the stray cats fed with any leftovers.

Most of the life boats on the channel were clinker built but some double diagonal and carvel built, mostly all double enders (sharp at each end) Most were made for just rowing, when the survivors of a shipwreck had several oars and usually a folding mast with gaff rigged sail to help them sail to land. We had to bribe a friendly shipwright to drill a hole in the stern for a propeller shaft this was a very skilled job. Teak, mahogany and pitch pine timber was readily available ensuring that working class men had the opportunity to own a tidy thirty foot boat, thanks to Wards and Vickers. We had an arrangement by bribing a man who worked nights at the fitting out berth by the High Level Bridge in Buccleuch dock. When the wind was blowing strong from the South he would throw overboard from the ship that was outfitting there, lengths of prime teak or pitch pine timber knowing that they would all end up at the Ferry Beach end of Devonshire dock. This is where we would be waiting with long spiked boat hook to lift the wood out, sliding it under the fence where our shed was at that time. Trouble was other boaters had similar agreements with other Vickers workers and sometimes it ended in fisticuffs, until the wood was shared out evenly! Such a lot of wood was always sought after when everybody owned wooden boats, it certainly caused some ill feeling among some people.

One incident over the wood still causes my old friend to chuckle, this happened early morning we had just pulled a twenty foot length of pitch pine out of the dock, congratulating each other that we were the only ones around. We heard an angry shout coming from the scrap yard at Low Road Bridge, under which our wood had just travelled. We saw that it was the scrap man who rented the land we were on to graze the rag and bone men's ponies. He lived in his caravan at the scrap yard believing that all the wood which drifted into the dock basin belonged to him. He owned a vicious guard dog that he let roam on his land to bolster his argument and deter wood collectors. Telling us to leave the wood on the grass or he would set the vicious dog loose, which was at that very moment straining at its lease, spittle was dripping from his fangs. Just the day before I was telling my mate about an article in the 'Readers Digest' about not running away from attacking dogs. You had to stand and face them down it said. My mate Brian said "You can fucking do what you like Norm I am running away now!" Ignoring the scrap man I called his bluff and continued to drag the wood towards the short distance to the shed. "You were warned!" shouted the scrap man and released the dog. My instinct was to run after my friend but knew that the dog was too fast for me to make the safety of the fence. Facing the dog I was crapping myself hoping that the advice given by the expert in the 'Readers Digest' was correct. The evil looking snarling brute ran towards me like 'The Hound Of The Baskervilles' shit my thoughts were, I am dead! The brute launched his self at me I put my arm up to protect my face, the dog grabbed my arm ripping the sleeve right off my brand new jacket. The man ran up to the dog put the lead back on, then scarpered back to his scrap yard realising he had gone too far this time. My mate was pissing himself laughing from over the fence, saying something about the article being a load of bollocks and that I should have followed him. The dog had to be put down a few weeks later having bit the local policeman. A row of teeth marks on my right arm was a reminder of the mad guard dog. Of course I terminated my subscription to 'Readers Digest'

Most engines were petrol, paraffin or if lucky a diesel engine out of a lorry, not many proper marine engines in those early days. All the paint and even the anti fouling paint was available to be pinched from Vickers, depending on what ship was on the slips at the time, so one could say our boating was subsidised. Some of the rowing life boats still had the brass or steel rowlocks, sets of oars and sometimes a lifting mast with canvas sails when purchased from the ship breakers. Some men put expensive stolen anti fouling paint in an old thermos flask and bought it out of the ship yard like that. A young lad coiled new galvanised chain around his waist for his boat anchor but got a little bit carried away with the weight. He walked out of the ship yard gates huddled in the middle of a crowd of mates, tripped over and fell, he could not get up again taking two of his mates to lift him onto his feet quickly before the Vickers security guards spotted him! It was instant dismissal of course if caught stealing.

The open boats were soon decked in, a handsome cabin and wheelhouse fitted, these boats were sometimes finished to boatyard standard such was the skill of the Vickers craftsmen. Every year on the shipyard's annual two weeks holiday several local boats made the trip to the Isle of Man, but first stopping off for a night out in the Ship Inn on Piel Island. These lads had been making this voyage in their converted lifeboats for years taking sacks of shackles, sacks of stainless steel rowlocks, all kinds of various fittings made when at work, all of which the Manxmen had trouble sourcing. That meant the Barrow lads not having to pay for their beer for quite a few nights out. The only boat on this journey that I recall coming to grief foundered under tow she was called the 'Gamecock,' which sank off Walney after the crew had been rescued by the lifeboat in very bad weather. There were several famous Morecambe bay prawners still afloat in Barrow such as the Empress, Ruby, Rose, Cricket, Queen Mary, Quest, and Skylark to name a few, my favourite was Empress a successful trawler who was always fished part time. She was fitted with a traditional capstan to haul in the trawl warps. A favourite place for this skipper to fish was in or off the Duddon estuary where he would consistently bring good catches of large plaice back to Barrow.

A strange incident happened to a prawner yacht in Morecambe bay many years ago. A well found prawner called 'Lady Anne' sailed from her home port of Fleetwood to visit a boat builder called John Ingram at Ferry beach Barrow. She then left to return home at two thirty in the afternoon passing the Barrow lifeboat out on exercise, who reported that her sails were drawing and the four men aboard seemed well. Four hours later the Lady Anne was seen to sail herself home up the Wyre channel into Fleetwood pier, then ground on a sandbank, then fill up and sink. At dusk on that October day she was reported by the Wyre lighthouse keepers to be sailing past, her mast damaged and sails trailing in the water with no signs of life aboard her. A Fleetwood steam trawler inward bound from the fishing grounds called the 'Agnes Wickfield,' also reported her sailing up the channel. Two fishermen managed to get aboard her before she filled with water and found no sign of life. The anxious relatives of the four men waited all night for news of any of the men being found, but after extensive searches, no sign of the men or their bodies were ever found. The Lady Anne was salvaged and put onto a mooring no one could understand how such a well found vessel could have lost all four crew overboard, continuing to sail across the bay as if she knew where she was going! No gale was blowing that day the wind was maybe strong enough to need a reef or two. Possibly being over canvassed caused her to broach tipping all the crew overboard, then right herself sailing on leaving the poor men to drown in the cold water. That was just one theory amongst many put forward over the years, but truth is nobody knows what really happened all those years ago. The treacherous Morecambe bay had yet again claimed more victims.

We finally managed to join the sailing club as full members and were given the old ferry Victorian ferry ticket office complete with slate roof, tiled floor even a coal fire. This was honestly better than our house which is why I spent every night of the year toasting crumpets on the fire, not wanting to go home. Most of the beach lads used to call in for a brew after working on their boats before heading off home. We learned how to mend nets and splice rope on dark winter nights, especially how to bullshit with the best of them. Many a huge rat that dared to lurk in our shed was dispatched using my air rifle. We must have been a nuisance for the old lady who lived in a converted ships lifeboat next to our shed. This lady was called 'Bertha' she owned a house nearby but loved to spend days in her lovely house boat. She also had use of a shed containing a stove, on a Sunday morning we could smell delicious scones cooked for her friends in the sailing club. We tried to keep our noise down but were young and Bertha was glad to see the back of us when the club made us move eventually to the opposite end of the beach. The house boat and Bertha are both long gone now, she was a great character but must have thought us young lads were a pain in the arse!

Down our beach then was a collection of these never to be forgotten men, the likes of which will never be seen again! One guy would pick whelks off the sewerage outfall by the shipyard obviously they grew fat and juicy feeding on the shite! We said it was unhealthy that he would poison himself, his answer to this was to put a raw whelk in his mouth then eat it!

One day in a shed on the bull nose a young lad was swinging a starting handle on a generator, trying his best to get it started, it fired and kicked back. We heard a crack and realized the lad had broken his arm on the starting handle, he was screaming in pain. An old fisherman dashed forward taking immediate control of the situation leading him along the quay then strangely down the stone steps leading to the tide. "What the fuck are you doing shouted the young lad I need a lift to hospital!"

"No need for bothering them at the hospital son, just dip your arm in the tide the saltwater will do it good!"

Another fly beggar would come into our shed and rummage around on a Sunday morning. Spotting a large solid brass semi rotary bilge pump under my work bench, ask us if he could give us something for it, being just what he had been looking for to install on his boat. Knowing I was a soft touch and would not charge him for it. Off he would go thanking me profusely, saying how ferry beach sailing club needed young lads like me what an asset to the club I was. An hour later to my surprise I saw it lying in Mr. Caines scrap van which always called down on Sunday mornings collecting scrap metal from our sheds. I had been well and truly conned and the old bugger that did me was stood at the bar in the 'Crow's Nest' having free drinks on me!

One fisherman was took short one day and decided he would pee into an empty milk bottle inside his shed, instead of a long walk to the toilet at the club house. Unfortunately he was surprised when somebody entered his shed unexpectedly. The poor man panicked swinging around breaking the glass bottle. He screamed out in pain, we ran in to see blood pouring down from his penis which had been badly cut by the broken glass. We wrapped it up with a large white towel which we found on his work bench. Driving him up to the hospital in a friend's vehicle he knew his penis obviously needed several stitches. The once white bath towel was bright red with his blood he looked an odd sight walking around holding a bloody bath towel to his groin. When the nurse persuaded him to reveal his manhood she gasped in astonishment, he was hung like a donkey! It seemed to take a hell of a lot of nurses to put the many stitches in that was required. My mate said they must have phoned their friends who were on tea breaks to come in and admire the stitching! I said they must have phoned the nurses that were at home on their days off, the amount that came in to look! He said that it was very embarrassing but could have been a lot worse it could have been cut off!

CHAPTER EIGHT

Leaving school in the sixties you were spoilt for career choices, we still had a decent merchant navy, deep water fishing fleet, and opportunities in the ship yard. In those far off days it seemed the world really was your oyster. Dad persuaded me to take an apprenticeship at Globe & Simpsons as an Auto electrician and diesel injection fitter. I was the only partner left in the dinghy now my other mates had found the joys of pub life. The only other apprentice at Globes decided to come in with me to try out the boating life.

With my fish money and wages I could now afford a clinker built twenty four foot fishing boat which had a proper marine engine inboard. The engine was petrol started then turned over when warm to TVO or (tractor vaporising oil) also it was handle start and called a 'Morris Navigator'. The boat was called 'Christopher' but soon renamed 'Provider' and registered for fishing, painted up she looked a picture. Only snag was the engine was a little temperamental, going through the Jubilee bridge spans on a raging spring tide was terrifying when the engine began to cough then splutter we had visions of being swept broadside onto the bridge supports and wrecked.

We learned another valuable lesson one day. At low tide we were giving the engine a run steaming fast under the bridge, failing to notice a very small pram dinghy with its occupant stood on a wooden beam at water level. He was spearing mullet which were abundant under the bridge. Our wash raced towards him sweeping around his waist causing him to lose his balance and fall in. My friend thought it was funny and started to laugh, he shouted to me above the noise of our engine that it was only big Mike he is a big prick, laughing even louder. Big Mike scrambled into his dinghy angrily waving a ham like huge fist at us which only made my friend laugh even louder. What we did not realise was how much sound carries over water but how quick we learned our lesson. We should have cut down our speed going through the bridge, certainly not have laughed at him, he had heard every word we said. Just as we were putting distance between us the engine started to cough and splutter, I realised we needed to get back to our mooring fast. Big Mike was furiously rowing towards his dad's thirty six foot long ferry boat intending to follow us, now I was worried. Mike had water rage written all over him, everyone knew he had anger management problems. Mike had just got back from a trip in the North Sea on a Lowestoft trawler always carried a sheaf knife and was not averse to using it. We had offended the wrong man and were going to pay the penalty.

Thinking that if we moored our boat up, we could quickly row ashore and leg it before Mike moored his dad's boat up. Mike started his boat's engine a big black cloud emitted from his exhaust. His boat appeared with a high bow wave showing he had the boat balls out. We had rowed ashore abandoning our dinghy thinking that we would still beat him, he still had to moor or anchor his boat up then row ashore. Only snag was he did not moor his boat up just ran it full speed up the beach narrowly missing our dinghy by inches, my mate said "Run like fuck or we are dead!" Never have I seen somebody run like my friend, he was out of sight in seconds, me with my limp was the sacrificial lamb ready for the slaughter. Turning around I looked into that mad bastard's eyes and knew what was coming. It was no good explaining that it was not me laughing. Losing track of time I took my punishment curled up in a tight ball on the beach while big Mike kicked me until his leg must have been very tired, then he used his fist. There is no doubt that I would have been in intensive care if a party of anglers had not come back from a fishing trip just when I needed them. They pulled him off with great difficulty, I was told it took about six of them, he was so angry. Two black eyes, several cracked ribs, bruises the size of grape fruit and a few days off work. I looked like a bus had run over me. It all could have been a lot worse, a lesson well learned about sound carrying over water. My only regret was that my friend could run faster than me, I did not blame him, Mike was built like a brick shit house, one thing was for sure I could not do anything manual except steer my boat for a while. Later on we became friends with Mike and we used to have a good laugh about it, well Mike did!

After some trips with the other fishing boats we were gaining a little bit more confidence at shooting and hauling the net. We decided to go on our first solo trip, our crewing days were over. The problem of where to fish is that in Morecambe bay at low tide the area exposed is about one hundred and twenty square miles of sand, mudflats, with deep and shallow channels cutting through. There are also deep holes big enough for a small boat to trawl around until the flood starts again, in these holes can be loads of fish which have drained off the high sand banks ready to be scooped up. The problem is finding these channels and holes without running aground ebbing out for the tide, leaving the day completely wasted.

The channels change constantly even daily, the tide rushing in faster than a horse can gallop was the local saying. Thousands of birds feed on these mud flats such as oyster catchers, eiders, curlews, lapwings, snipe, various gulls and herons etc. feeding on seed mussel, cockles, sea snails and lugworm. At first glance the vast expanse of sand looks devoid of life but you would be wrong. The bay is maybe three times more fertile than the best farmland, with nutrients constantly washing in from rivers and erosion. Underneath the sand are millions of lugworms, rag worms and tiny pink shells. In the shallow pools are sand hoppers, shrimps, flatfish such as plaice, turbot, lemon soles lying just under the sand with only their eyes protruding. Most deadly of all is the poisonous spines of the weaver fish which are extremely painful, we were taught to pee on the affected place to help alleviate the pain, if you cannot pee, use fresh water. We had to avoid towing our trawl into wrecks, rough ground, old schooner anchors all sorts of obstructions that will rip open a net and ruin the days fishing, all experience only comes with time. Our friends had shown us a few clear tows in the middle of Walney channel and one in the middle of Morecambe bay it was the latter we chose for our maiden trip.

Up at the crack of dawn on a perfect calm morning had us rowing aboard 'Provider' very excited at the prospects of a large catch of plaice. The engine started for once easily and seemed to run smoothly as if being a good omen. Casting off we steamed under the Jubilee Bridge that joins Barrow to Walney Island setting a course for Morecambe bay on the ebb tide. Bacon sizzling in the frying pan the kettle whistling, what more could you ask? Passing Walney lighthouse I changed course to go against the outgoing tide flowing like a mill race out of the bay, slowly steered onto my marks where a channel would be left at low tide. We dropped the anchor waiting until the run of tide eased off and the tops of the sandbanks started to appear, I could see we were right where we wanted to be. The rise and fall in our area is over thirty feet on spring tides a massive movement of water. Morecambe bay at low tide is a vast expanse of sand banks interspersed with channels and pools in which lots of fish may or not drain into. A very dangerous place indeed, that needed to be treated with a great deal of respect. The run had eased now so starting up the engine we threw over the trawl net starting to tow the net slowly up and down the large pool we were in. The maximum depth of water was about six feet so we could see the orange net floats on the surface and the sand kicked up by the two otter boards which held the mouth of the net open. The water was like gin, by looking over the bow of the boat you could see the large flatfish scooting right and left as we disturbed them, like looking into a giant aquarium.

Well it seems to be going well the net was shot away without us getting it around our propeller. We anchored in the right place in the middle of the channel I think we may have landed on a fish shop here lads! My boat only drew two feet of water so when we ran aground on the sand we could go over the side just pushing her off and carry on towing the trawl. After one hour towing up and down covering all the area, we were convinced that we might not have enough fish boxes to hold all our fish. Time to haul the net in now I decided, we knocked the engine out of gear starting hauling a warp each, the water was so clear you could see the huge plaice with big red spots lying in the wings of the net. "My God we have a plaster of fish here, shake them all down to the cod end like we have been taught, we do not want to lose any!" In my head was a pound sign, the money already was in the bank! As the net wings were pulled in and stowed on the side deck we continued to shake loads of fish downwards towards the narrow cod end where all the fish collected. We would use a block and tackle off the top of the mast to lift the heavy weight of fish onboard. A very large salmon (the first I had seen) was shaken down, some large skate, this was fantastic. I felt like a king, all this and I was just turned sixteen a part time trawler skipper. All of us dressed like adverts for tins of tuna fish, long black oilskins, black wellies and black sou wester's, we certainly looked like trawlermen from a distance.

They say that pride comes before a fall that is what happened to me, suddenly it dawned on me that all our beautiful fish were going straight through the cod end swimming back to freedom. My first idea was a large rock must have ripped a big hole in the net but that theory was quickly dispelled when I got the cod end aboard the boat. There was not a rip I wish it was. We had not even tied the cod end up in the first place!

Recriminations followed each of us blamed the other. The bottom line was it was my fault, being the skipper it was down to me, some fisherman I turned out to be! Peed off is not the right word, I felt awful we had just thrown away a lot of money, all the fish was prime stuff and a lot of it. Another valuable lesson in fishing you might not get a chance like this again. Due to me not checking all the gear myself it had cost me money more importantly I had lost my crew their wages! The tide was flooding in now our chance had gone, a long steam home with plenty of time to ponder my mistake. One thing was for sure we would not be broadcasting about what went on this day around Ferry beach for a long time.

Many other mishaps would happen in the excitement of learning the art of trawling, like getting a net around the propeller, running aground, getting the net caught around a wreck, even throwing the complete set of gear over forgetting to have it tied onto the boat. When we ran aground the deck brushes would be used to scrub the weed off the bottom of the boat and we would wait patiently for the tide to come back in. Sometimes after a full day's fishing, we would anchor Provider in Bass pool which had Piel Island on one side and the south end of Walney Island on the other, where sat the lighthouse. My friend Peggy would become the only female lighthouse keeper in the country. Her sister Ella held the post until 1967 then Peggy took over and was appointed principal keeper in 1975 when she married Ken who happened to be my boss at Globe & Simpsons.

The lighthouse was built of stone quarried from Overton in Lancashire and bought to the site by ship. The tower is seventy feet high and visible from Blackpool across the bay. There are two cottages attached to the lighthouse where the keeper and assistants live. When Peggy came to live there the water supply was collected rain water, the cottages candle lit. Around the lighthouse is a huge gullery and a rabbit warren, an oyster farm uses the water in the old gravel pits nowadays to good advantage.

Of course now the light is fully automated and the lovely cottages sold off to private buyers, one on the market presently for £250,000 the end of another era. Back in Bass pool we anchored the boat then rowed ashore to take Peggy a feed of fish. Walking up the beach we usually stumbled across some useful trawl floats or trawl netting washed up in the last storm so kept our eyes open. Crossing the sand dunes suddenly we heard a sharp crack a rabbit quietly grazing in front of us suddenly shot up in the air with a neat bullet hole in its head. A loud voice shouted 'Pick the rabbit up and bring it to the house will you?' I looked around and realized the voice came from the gallery of the lighthouse it was Peggy sorting out her rabbit dinner. The fish were exchanged for a brace of rabbits, a large slice of fruitcake plus mug of sweet tea. Peggy used to do quite a bit of fishing keeping their boat in the sheltered lagoon nearby, after a good yarn it was time to row aboard and make for home.

Sometimes when I visited Peggy she would be swinging on a bosun's chair halfway up the tower slapping on white paint helped by her sister.

Peggy painted her beloved lighthouse eleven times to my knowledge. The same job these days dictate the tower surrounded with scaffold and several tradesmen doing the job thanks to health and safety rules.

Her husband Ken had a shed stacked high with beach combed stuff collected after storms had bought the booty ashore on his remote beach, mooring buoys, rope, trawl nets, lengths of hard wood timber, several dinghy's an 'Aladdin' cave of treasure. Another regular visitor was my friend George the skipper of Barrow pilot boat for many years, he moored his boat up to the old sand and gravel pier in Bass pool, either the 'Irene Allen', 'Albacore' or 'Argus' depending what was being used at Heysham, George worked both ports. While he was waiting for the pilot to undock from Barrow George would visit Peggy for tea and her famous fruit cake. In the early days of learning how to be a pilot boat deckhand the old skipper would cover up the windows in the wheel house, to test George on his skill in taking the boat down channel out to sea using a compass and clock timings, all the timed courses written down to memorize in case of thick fog. Also to learn how to box a compass, all before plotters and radars were used on small boats, he was a proper sailor.

Peggy's father, sister and brother in law all helped to keep the light guiding shipping away from the treacherous sands and shallows on the approaches to Barrow. All this is history now Peggy MBE and her beloved husband Ken have all passed over the bar now. Peggy was tough, I recall calling one day with some fish, not noticing the iron spike sticking out of a plank of wood that Ken had dragged up from the beach earlier leaving it by the gate to the cottage. Stepping on it, the sharp spike went clean through my foot. The spike protruded out of the top of my wellington boot pinning my foot to the plank like a butterfly in a glass case, I could feel my boot filling up with blood. The pain was so bad I could feel myself feeling faint when looking down at my foot.

Peggy took control at once told me to lean on her then pull my foot off the plank quickly while she stood on it. I felt no choice but to do as she said, you never argued with Peggy!

"Empty the blood out of your boot down the drain" Peggy said, then washed the foot in a dish, bandaged it, that was that!

"Right I am off to clean the lamp room put that plank of wood spike down Norm you know what Kens like, the silly bugger will probably stand on it one silly bugger today is enough!" My wellingtons were brand new now one would leak!

Arriving down Ferry beach to go on another fishing trip my boat was missing, scratching my head I wandered if she had broken her mooring and been washed out of the north end of Walney then out to sea.

"She has not gone anywhere Norm the tip of the mast is jutting out of the water she has sunk!" my crew said. Bloody hell that is all I need knowing all the work involved in restoring her back to a seaworthy condition entailed. At low tide we bailed her out and looked underneath to find out what had caused her to sink, a sharp stone had punctured the planking on her bilge making a small hole in her, she must have sat on it at low tide when she ebbed out last. Quickly nailing on a temporary patch we worked her up the beach to the high water mark on the flood tide. Using a borrowed set of chain blocks she was pulled up higher than the tide would ever reach for the next month, while repairs were carried out.

The engine was lifted out using a set of scaffold tubes set up over the cockpit and a chain block again. We borrowed a four wheel bogey and the engine was wheeled into the shed for an overhaul. With the engine out of the boat and all the floor boards removed, to my horror I realised about twenty ribs needed replacing plus a couple of short planks. This was well out of our league, we did not know a shipwright well enough to ask or have enough money to pay anybody to help us.

An old timer came to our rescue, for the price of some cigarettes and a few beers he said he would tell us what to do if we did the hard work. We had no choice so set to work buying the timber for the ribs, short planks, copper rivets, and rooves. Also we constructed a steamer box to soften the ribs while bending them to the shape of the hull. Over the coming evenings and weekends we learned the art of taking out rotten ribs replacing with new, one of us outside one inside the hull, putting in copper nails snipping off just enough nail to rivet over with a ball hammer. We became quite good and our old friend was pleased with us, many packets of fags plus a shed load of beer money later, the short planks were in, the engine installed, the boat was painted up a treat ready for sea again. A few more fishing trips and a bit more money saved, I decided to part with my first proper boat to buy a better vessel, so put Provider up for sale in the 'Fishing News'. A young lad bought her to fish the Solway Firth out of a little harbour called Harrington. We borrowed a boat escorting the Provider out of the north end of Walney channel which was a shorter route when heading northwards up the coast. We watched my old boat until she disappeared out of our sight into the mist, I hoped the new owner got as much fun out of her as I had.

We had a spell of cockling in Morecambe bay at the Rampside end of the estuary to get some extra cash. We took them around the local pubs in half a crown bags, they sold really well. We enjoyed following the tide out early mornings, watching the sunrise on a beautiful summer's dawn the vast expanse of Morecambe bay spread out before us. We did not use jumbo boards but a hand craam a small three pronged fork with the last inch bent over at right angles. Usually we made a wooden handle about a foot in length. The cockles were usually only half an inch under the surface of the sand so easy to flick out. We had quite a long walk back to our vehicle so only collected a basket full each. The price of cockles soared in later years that encouraged illegal picking without permits and the unscrupulous gang masters moved in.

This bay was the scene of a tragic cockling disaster in February 2004 when a gang of Chinese pickers were caught out on the sands by the strong tides, cutting off their escape. This was on the Morecambe side of the bay off Hest Bank twenty three cockle pickers including three women were drowned. The gang masters who organised it had no real local knowledge of how dangerous the bay could be or cared, these poor people paid the ultimate price. These cockle pickers were illegal immigrants mainly from the Fujian province of China, were untrained, inexperienced and desperately poor. British cocklers returning to shore on the same dark, windy evening attempted to warn the Chinese group by tapping their watches and trying to speak with them to no avail. One of the gang masters was jailed and lessons were learned, new tighter regulations were bought out for health and safety procedures for anyone who was granted a licence in the future. One thing is for sure the bay is unforgiving to anybody who makes mistakes, you will not get a second chance, and there is no substitute for local knowledge!

CHAPTER NINE

The man who taught us how to repair clinker built boats owned a smart clinker built, double ender (pointed at each end) ex lifeboat that he had converted into a fishing trawler. She had pitch pine laid deck, a centre wheelhouse, wheel steering and a powerful diesel engine. The trawl net still had to be pulled in by hand no winch or capstan had been fitted, this was not too great a hardship as we mostly only had to trawl in shallow water to catch enough fish in those days. Her name was 'Mischief' and she had certainly lived up to her name with the previous owner over the years he had owned her. This boat was very strongly reinforced, built like a battleship, full length railway line bolted along the keel and full length nine by three pitch pine timbers bolted on the inside. The engine was started with a key no more swinging a bloody starting handle on a cold winter's morning.

The first day we tried the boat we were cruising off Walney Island coming across a huge expensive catamaran disabled with crab pot ropes around both propellers, with not a breath of wind to sail. We tied alongside and I volunteered to go over the side with a sharp knife to cut the rope off, with a line tied around my waist the props were soon cleared, good job the sea was calm. The owner was so pleased he did not need to call out the Barrow lifeboat he gave me a cheque for the sum of twenty five pounds, which was a lot of money in those days. The cuts I sustained off the sharp edges of the propellers to my fingers, the blood running out of them splashing onto his lovely boat must have made him feel generous. None of us would ever refuse to help anyone in difficulty. If I could not clear his propellers we would have towed him into Barrow and put him on a safe mooring. After using up all his plasters and shaking my hand, the owner of that beautiful boat pointed her in the direction of Ireland and motored away, giving us a last cheery wave.

Four in the morning saw us rolling on a lazy swell a mile off Black Combe a Cumbrian mountain. We were fishing in only thirty feet of water trying to locate a huge mackerel shoal. Only using hand lines with ten feathers catching five or six every time, we soon had four baskets of the lovely fish. How soon the colours fade but unlike the ones bought in fish mongers ours would be only three hours old when landed. We sold the mackerel at five in a bag for half a crown in the local pubs that night.

A free bag for the landlord and it secured access to his pub, in those times carpets in the bar were unusual, wooden floors and usually a big roaring fire greeted the pub regulars. Most weekends a sizable fleet of boats would be steaming down channel to try and earn some money to eke out their wages, each skipper would have his favourite place to fish. Thanks to the shipyard most of the boats were very well equipped. Some boats possessed the odd stainless steel anchor, shafts, propellers, ropes, shackles and paint, just about anything could be obtained if you knew the right people. All of the boat owners had a boat shed full to the brim with gear, chairs and brewing facilities were essential so that a good crack could be had when it became too dark to work outside. Wooden boats were labour intensive so Ferry beach was busy all the time, some of the lads involved in major projects. Most boats were ex lifeboats mostly double ended, a shipwright sometimes put in a transom stern (square stern) a very skilled job. There were double diagonal hulls, clinker built and carvel hull types mostly bought from Wards for a pound a foot, usually the boats were about thirty foot long. Most conversions done on Ferry beach were so skilfully done that you would think a top class boat yard had done the work. There were many fitters or engineers from the shipyard who could help in the installation of a new engine. On our channel were several famous Morecambe bay prawners or half deckers, some converted into smart yachts the others fishing trawlers, the most successful at bringing back good catches was the thirty two foot Empress. The fuel was only a shilling a gallon and most boat sheds had a large capacity tank or a forty gallon drum inside.

When a new ship was being launched into Walney channel, massive amounts of timber which held them upright would come floating free, then getting caught in the strong tide be washed out of the north end of Walney, far out to sea to be lost. This timber was very expensive to replace, and Vickers shipbuilders wanted it back at all cost to use again for the next launch. Which is where my neighbour helped me out, he had the contract for years to organise getting the wood back to Vickers, he would choose about ten boats with reliable engines hiring us for the day to retrieve this wood. This hire was very lucrative for the lucky few, not only did we receive the equivalent of a week's wages but could pinch prime pieces of timber to stow in our cabins out of sight! Hard luck if you had fallen out with Fred you were not asked again for the next few launches. On the morning of the launch Fred would motor around early in his lovely clinker built ex naval launch. This was powered by a powerful Perkins P6 diesel engine. Fred sailed alongside each of the hired boats dropping off a sack of heavy steel 'u' shaped staples and a large coil of new sisal rope. This timber recovery job was very dangerous, Health and Safety officials these days would be appalled at the danger we were in!

Soon as possible after the newly launched ship had been bought to a halt mid channel, Fred's boat would take a line to one of the waiting Liverpool tugs. Then the tow into the dock to the fitting out berth could commence. All this had to be carried out swiftly and efficiently while a short period of slack water was on, before the vicious ebb tide had not yet started. The secret was to get the biggest rafts of timber first and towed into the slipways quickly, where a huge winch on land would take your tow rope and start hauling the timber above the high water mark. Doing this fast would impress Fred and guarantee you a place on the next launch! Sometimes we would be so keen we strayed too near the launched ship before the wood had time to come to the surface, suddenly a huge piece of timber would shoot up like a rocket, emerging only feet away from our boat. The real danger was putting the boat alongside the baulks of timber in a ripping tide, and leaning over the side with your crew holding onto your legs to reach the wood. You had a two pound hammer in one hand, an end of rope with a knot tied and holding a large steel staple in the other hand. Then you had to hammer the staple into very hard wood over the rope, trying not to hit your fingers whilst hanging upside down. In winter your fingers would be numb with the cold water. You had to do a good job otherwise the weight of wood being towed against a rip tide would pull out the staple and then you would have to steam around starting all over again.

Looking back I cannot believe the risks we were all taking, it was certainly a health and safety nightmare. You could not wear lifejackets they were too bulky you needed to be unrestricted, some of the small boats had very low freeboards so made it easier to lean over the side. Sometimes the pieces of timber were so huge, you just jumped off the boat onto the wood with your gear, and quickly hammered in two or three staples over the rope to make really sure it did not pull out. This was really scary a lot of the big pieces of wood would be coated with thick tallow to enable the ship to slide down the slipway easier, ensuring it was very greasy, really easy to lose your footing. Looking back if anybody had slipped into the tide overboard it would have been curtains in those turbulent waters.

Vickers always put a notice in the local paper before a launch to warn all the boat owners to move their yachts out of the fairway. Many yachtsmen still left their boat on the mooring making our wood recovery even more awkward. Also until all the timber had passed under the Jubilee Bridge we had the added danger of being dragged onto the bridge supports where the tide swill was horrendous. All our masts had to be removed or laid flat to enable us to pass through the middle of the bridge. Our engines in the early days were not as reliable, some of the small boats still had petrol paraffin and you had to use full power all the time causing the added problem of overheating. If this happened you tied alongside another boat or picked up a mooring for a while. Sometimes the large rafts of timber would wrap around a yacht left on her mooring, even after everyone had been warned to shift their boats previously by Vickers. The weight of the wood either broke the mooring chain or sank the boat, either way the shipyard took no responsibility. Vickers sent out teams of men and wagons to collect any timber that washed into the channel sides. They kept an eye open for anybody that rowed out in small boats towing in choice wood for their own use. Most of the boats stacked up prime pieces of wood into their cabins, to be unloaded later that day when it was safe to do so. The channel was filled with thousands of whitewood wedges only fit for burning on the fire, days after these would be washing up on the coastline for miles around. The ebb tide flowed for two hours north then turned running south, this is when the timber towing boats had the tide with them, helping them to get back to the Vickers slipways easier.

All the moorings in Walney channel have been in place for many years and some passed from father to son. Some are sold when the boat owner gives up and retires, as long as the centre fairway is kept clear for Barrow lifeboat or the dock launches the harbour authority leaves the policing to the local sailing clubs. This must be one of the rare places where boat moorings are free the downside is all the moorings were taken long ago.

Over the years we worked on all kinds of launches, huge tankers, passenger liners, destroyers, nuclear submarines all exciting times for young lads hoping to make a living out of our small boats. The day of the launches the shipyard brass band played, crowds would cheer, the tugs and small craft would blow their horns. There was a great shared atmosphere, all the workers and their families proud of the craftsmanship in our small town of Barrow. Sometimes the wind would rise at high tide and start gusting very strongly, then the pilot in overhaul charge would cancel the launch leaving it for the next day's high water. When this occurred we then received an extra day's fee, this did not happen very often. Sometimes the Queen would attend the launch so the pressure was on to make it happen come what may!

Fred was always good to me, he had watched me grow up from a baby, him also living in Glasgow Street meant we saw a lot of each other. He hired my boat several times for interesting other charters. For several days my boat with a few others were loaded up with marker buoys that had flags attached, each boat had a cargo of different coloured ones, at a given time and place dropped them into the tide around the launch ways in the channel. All this was filmed from the top of one of the giant cranes jibbed out over the channel. The survey was used to check the tidal flow for the next set of launches and turned out to be a good earner for us. When he was not hiring his boat to the shipyard, Fred ran a one man building business from a lockup in Glasgow Street. He was a good sailor, builder and gentleman.

In between our adventures with the wood recovery we carried on fishing, occasionally catching a lobster in our trawl net, we each took turns to keep them. Sometimes you had a small one, occasionally a giant one, all depending on how lucky you were when it was your turn. One day I took home to mother a huge one, all the Ferry beach men agreed that they had not seen the like before. Proud as punch I carried it home in a sack and gave it to mother to cook later for our supper. Feeling tired after a day hauling in ropes I went for a snooze in the armchair. I was awakened shortly out of my slumber by an unearthly screeching. Leaping out of the chair I ran into the kitchen to see mum's cat tearing around the room dragging the huge lobster behind him, his tail firmly clasped in a huge claw. The cats eyes were bulging and his fur stood on end. Before I could do anything to help the cat, the lobster's claw cut right through his tail releasing Tom which promptly shot straight out of the open window, leaving behind four inches of tail. Just then mother came in saw the lobster on the floor and her cat's tail in his claw and nearly fainted. "I only went out for a minute the lobster looked dead so I left it on the draining board, bloody hell its eaten my cat, get me a cup of tea, four sugars quick!"

Poor Tom he did not come home for two weeks.

Mother would not throw any food away that might do to feed stray cats or seagulls, all the other house wives in the back street used to complain about the seagull shit on their washing, she just told them to bugger off and mind their own business. When the stray cats and seagulls saw me coming down the street carrying a bag I would be like the piped piper, the crowd of cats meowing, rubbing against my legs, the usual half dozen seagulls squawking above my head, it was bloody embarrassing! To solve the problem I filleted the fish on the boat leaving mum no fish heads or offal to chuck on our shed roof, peace was restored with mum's neighbours.

My crewmate came down to the boat one day with a young ginger haired kid, he was about seven or eight years old visiting him from Manchester. We were to take him out for a day's cod fishing off 'Bar' buoy. "Bloody hell" I said "he is a dead ringer for you Brian" both had ginger hair and were like clones of each other, he turned out to be my friend's cousin. We anchored off the buoy in a heavy swell I thought any minute this young lad who was called Mick, would be sea sick. We gave him a fishing rod, put two hooks on, baited up with mussel and told him to strike upwards if he got any bites. He sat on the stern end of the boat a pie in one hand, jamming himself in tightly so he did not get thrown overboard. He certainly looks the part your Mick I remarked as his rod tip started to bend. Mick started to reel in, two fine codling were on his line, beginners luck we all thought. We three adults had not even a bite between us, Mick reeled in again with two more codling. I can see him now in my mind a huge grin on his face and his nose running like a tap, not believing his luck! End of the day Mick had a heap of codling to take home we all had not even a nibble between us, that young lad grew up to be the world famous 'Mick Hucknall' of Simply Red fame a good fisherman and even greater singer!

Seventeen and still not owning a fishing boat big enough to go full time fishing on was getting me down a bit, the impatience of youth. I decided to put Mischief up for sale. Taking some leave from work my friend's van was put to good use and we set off to tour around Scotland, looking at every harbour for a suitable boat to buy. Not a port was missed our search went as far as John O' Croats, lovely boats but way out of my price range, I was very disappointed but we had a great adventure sleeping in the back of the van each night. We met some real Scottish characters and had a few sessions in the quaint little harbour side pubs, we were made very welcome. We were offered many a crewing position on some fine looking boats but always turned them down. We nearly became residents of Oban a local man had just bought a beautiful Norwegian style trawler built like a battleship, he offered us permanent berths in her. She was to fish for prawns the money was very good at that time. A bonus was we could live aboard the boat which would have cost us nothing. The temptation to stay was great but I still wanted to have the excitement of being skipper with my own boat.

CHAPTER TEN

On our way home from Scotland we decided to drop into Maryport to see what this run down harbour had to offer. We parked on the quayside and sitting in the mud below us was a thirty two feet long Morecambe bay prawner. Hell she did look rough and battered by one too many storms but straight away I could see potential, she was the right size for me to fish her full time. Truth is I was getting a bit desperate and disillusioned after so many boats being out of my price range in Scotland, so was lowering the bar. The boat did not even have a name plate on her, was painted white, her hull was streaked in rust stains. A capstan winch was on the fore deck in front of the original mast, she had a small wheelhouse and a deep cockpit. On the huge counter stern lay a trawl net, with a huge tiller to steer her with. This was going to be my boat I just knew. Finding out who the owner was then getting him down straight away to show me around, I prodded and poked about. She had a two berth cabin forward heated by a small coal fire, midships was a six cylinder Perkins P6 diesel engine (out of a lorry) much over powered but fuel was cheap at one shilling a gallon. My mates said not to touch her with a barge pole she was buggered, but being impulsive I asked the man how much he wanted for her. He gave me the usual bullshit about this vintage fine boat will take you safely anywhere in any storm the engine will never let you down blah, blah!

"Cut the crap how much will you take for cash?" I said.

"Five hundred pounds" was the answer.

"My only offer is two hundred and fifty pounds shake on it or I walk away!"

He shook hands with me the deal was done, I trusted him and was the new proud owner of the prawner. I had dreamt about this moment all these years. Knowing it was stupid not to have had a sail in her, hear the engine going, or have inspected the hull. The tide was out the owner said he had another cash buyer coming down later that day. I was naive falling for the sales pitch and had to have the boat come what may. A fisherman down Ferry beach had promised to buy Mischief for three hundred pounds so there was a bit of spare money in the kitty. The next weekend saw me boarding the Barrow train heading for Maryport, carrying a bloody great anchor plus coil of new rope, all my friends carrying various bags of gear.

The 'Misty Morn' was the name I gave her she looked beautiful to me, floating on a calm dock the sun shining down on us. The man was paid in cash and seemed to have a relieved smile on his face when he counted his money. We all climbed down the ladder and the man started up the engine, we all started coughing when the exhaust fume cloud enveloped us, but when she warmed up it seemed alright. We all shook hands with the Maryport man, we cast off and headed through the harbour entrance, me with my fingers crossed!

The forecast was good the kettle was on, my beautiful prawner sat like a duck in the water. Until I increased the engine revolutions, then boat's counter was drawn deeper into the sea and a flow of seawater poured in through the stern. "The fucking boats sinking already turn around now and drop us off!" shouted the crew. "Look!" I said "When I knock the revs off the leak slows down." Panic over we carried on southwards down the coast, passing the ports of Workington and Whitehaven, then the huge sandstone cliffs of St. Bees Head where a fleet of trawlers were working off shore. The engine was running well and we were making good progress.

I was feeling a little more confidant now but had to pump out the water sloshing around in the bilges regularly. She was an old vintage boat after all, and if I did not want to borrow money from the bank, I would have to put up with the problems of a vintage historical craft. We steamed into Barrow channel still in one piece, and laid her up on the high tide mark, we then fitted a pair of wooden legs on her to hold her upright when the tide ebbed. Whilst the tide was in we went home for a wash and dinner, looking forward to inspecting the boats bottom to see the condition. This was something I should have done before buying her. Not many old wooden boats were insured in those days it was far too expensive and most would not pass a vigorous survey anyway.

When I got back to the boat it was obvious that the local experts had beat me to it, the bottom was full of nicks where knives had been pushed in, even the odd screwdriver. At least one of the old shipwrights had the balls to say "It is fucked son!" to my face. Fair enough I had never before seen a lead patch the size of the one that covered the underneath of Misty Morn's counter, plus the several smaller lead and copper patches that were tacked on randomly. I could have earned a few bob selling the copper patches to the scrap man! The winter months would be spent working on her and repairing what I could, it was a fact that the biggest critics in the boat club were the ones that had the most expensive boats, but used them the least! Well I gave them something new to talk about while they were drinking their tea and dunking biscuits in the club house.

Over the next few months small pockets of rot were removed and new wood put in place. The large patch under the counter was never touched I just did not have the balls to remove it, frightened by what might be revealed! She looked a picture with a new coat of paint and anti fouling on the bottom. Seventeen years old and I now made the decision to pack my apprenticeship in and look for a higher paid job in order to get the boat ready for full time fishing. My boss Ken tried his best to get me not to leave but my mind was made up. Looking back we were lucky to have a free choice of what boat to buy and what species of fish to catch. To take our chances using our own judgment, free from outside petty official influences. We could not have had all our adventures nowadays with all the EEC rules and regulations, fishermen's lives are swamped by petty regulations. Fishermen are getting fewer, while the office bound pen pushers in Brussels dealing with fisheries polices, are being increased. This does not seem fair to me the United Kingdom should take back all responsibility for the fishery in our own waters, maybe then all our harbours will come to life again. There are enough rich grounds around our coast to sustain a thriving industry once more instead we allow other countries to plunder our fish stocks, after they have decimated their own local waters.

Morecambe Bay prawner Empress at Ferry Beach

Norm holding cod with Brian

Fruitful still fishing today in the Orkney Islands

Piel Castle and Bass Pool where I was stuck in sinking sand

Walney Lighthouse

Seal waving flipper at us as we passed

Trawler Stephil

Tak Lift crane lifting Stephil off the seabed

Mike, Stewart and Brian on board the Melanie Jane

Melanie Jane

Barrow Streets dominated by the huge bulk of a Trident submarine

Bucket dredger Europe

Gary with a grand-dad lobster he returned to the sea

Duddon Inshore Rescue our village lifeboat

Easter Morn

Easter Morn

CHAPTER ELEVEN

S itting in front of the careers officer at the Labour Exchange I received another lecture on the stupidity of giving up a great career and I should change my mind, not a chance! "What's the highest paid job on your books then?" I asked.

"We have the North Walney Sand & Gravel quarry we keep sending men there and they do not last the day, it seems to be a bit like the Wild West, the money is good though."

"That will do me, will you tell them I am on my way?"

"See you back here tomorrow!" he said laughing.

"You will not!" was my reply.

Jumping on my pushbike I peddled against a howling westerly gale to the sand quarry thinking at least coming home the wind would be behind me. I was exhausted, when I took my first look at the site nearly turning around and going back to the careers office. The sand quarry was next to Vicker's tip but they both blended in, spotting a tiny shed I reported to the foreman for an interview.

The foreman said "Are you punctual and willing to do anything?"

"Yes" I said.

"Start now then, no buggers turned up again today, come with me I will show you around."

Not even a medical!

The site consisted of Second World War concrete sheds used for parking the loading shovel in at night, sheds housing the huge diesel generator for powering a sand drying plant and a gravel crushing plant. "Your mess room" he pointed to a railway cattle truck propped up on baulks of timber. "The last shed used for the mess room we set fire to it to kill all the rat's nesting underneath, toilet needs are old news papers and a short walk into the sand dunes. There is a public toilet at Earnsie bay but it is a mile away so I do not encourage anybody to use it, we cannot keep stopping the plant while people nip off!"

The reason why nobody ever stayed here was becoming apparent. Inside our cabin was old car seats spread around, off the tip I was told, a propane heater that heated our kettle, a five gallon container for our fresh water filled at the tap outside the public toilets once a day.

All in all a rough place to work but I looked forward to the higher wages, and soon I could go fishing when I bought all the gear I needed.

The first week the management bought an old land rover to use as a taxi to try and encourage the workers to stay, it only partly worked half the men still did not turn up. The man who cycled in one hour early six mornings a week to start up all the plant left suddenly. I was given the task of starting up the generator and doing his old job. The various different plants were started up then a walk by torchlight in the dark to the ponds that had been dug out for the huge water pumps was required.

My wages were enormous with all the extra overtime compared to my old apprentice wage. The foreman thought I was a great lad, always punctual, and thanks to my boat experience could use a set of spanners, making myself very useful. I would stay behind at night fixing broken plant, often replacing brake pads in the various vehicles the fine sand wore everything out constantly. This foreman fitter showed me how to weld and use burning gear, drive the loading shovel, also the huge tractor and trailer used for bringing excavated sand and gravel from the workings further north of our site. Eventually mastering the brand new dragline used for digging out the spoil we used, that is why the huge lagoons were created and now classified as a special nature reserve for natterjack toads and birds.

After a week or so I found a short cut to the quarry across the small private Vickers airfield, only used occasionally by small passenger aircraft on shipyard business. The security men soon got used to me cycling across early morning. In winter sheep were bought down from the high fells to graze the airfield for many years and the shepherd lived in a caravan, the control tower told him when a plane was due so he could move his sheep. I ran into one of his sheep now and again in the pitch black winter mornings when my bike lights were not working, nearly breaking my neck as I flew over my handle bars head first, cursing the bloody sheep.

The quarry had a new sand drying plant consisting of a huge steel cylinder fitted with a flame thrower. This was fuelled by diesel oil which was vaporised, then lit with a paraffin soaked rag on a short pole, which ignited with a great roar and was hellish noisy. The sand fed into it from a hopper onto a conveyor belt. The sand was delivered from north of the site at the lagoons, where the dragline worked none stop stock piling sand and cobbles to feed the hungry plant. The man who passed the early morning start on to me said the old war sheds were haunted, he was not sad to pack the job in, I laughed at him thinking he had too much imagination he was only trying to scare me.

When I arrived early in the morning in the teeth of an Irish Sea full blown gale, rain blowing horizontal, hearing the wind howling around the old sheds, loose roofing tins rattling and banging it was eerie. I always felt a presence close by me, felt the hairs on the back of my neck rise, it certainly scared me, especially in the generator shed, often seeing a tall figure standing in the far corner. My hands would shake as I checked the generator for oil and water by the light of a dim torch. Seeing the figure standing in the corner sometimes made me panic, often making me start the generator engine straight away without doing any checking, not being able to stand the tension a moment longer. Gratefully I relished the sudden glow of the lights, a quick tour around checking the various equipment, starting up the crushing and washing plants, then walking by torchlight to the deep ponds to start the water pumps going.

This old timer I met told me about a war time romance on the airfield between a pilot and a young lady who worked in the control tower. She was waiting for her pilot to return after having been killed in an air accident. Hearing this story made me feel a little better about the presence I was seeing thinking it was not malevolent. After all the plant was running smoothly I would walk up the hopper loading ramp, looking out to sea to see if any trawlers were making their way home to Fleetwood, on a calm morning you might see the deck lights of the inshore boats fishing close inshore. About this time I would see the headlights of the firm's land rover and wonder who had not turned up for work that day, it was a rare day when you had a full work force, meaning the few that were in had to do multi tasking, some men moaned and groaned but I found it interesting.

The dragline operator had the most skilled job, we needed just clean sand for the sand dryer, a half and half mix of cobbles/sand for sharp sand for concreting and clean sand for builders for cementing. A correct mixture for each hopper made the plant operators job a lot easier, if too wet sand was delivered to the sand dryer you had to constantly adjust the flame using massive amounts of diesel fuel and the sand could be too burnt for use in Vickers foundry, or if the screens were not checked regularly for holes allowing small stones into the sand an explosion might occur at the foundry. Nobody ever wanted to run this plant, the noise, the heat, and the constant fuel adjustments. The fine sand got up your nose and in your eyes, you would be frequently coughing sand balls up, to sum this job up it was the pits! Nobody in their right minds would do this job, maybe a new starter until he sussed it out.

When no wind blew, the fine sand drifted down on everyone coating the area with a fine layer like talcum powder, then everybody was in a foul mood, everybody's eyes would be blood shot. The fine sand even seeped into our (cattle wagon) mess room getting into our sandwiches making them feel gritty between our teeth. We looked forward to a good Irish Sea breeze to blow the dust over the nearby airfield away from us. Our access road had to be cleared regularly of sand drifts using the loading shovel, a job I particularly enjoyed not yet possessing a driving licence, seems one was not required on private land in those days.

The quarry made the most profit from the high quality foundry sand we produced. A small enclosed conveyor system lifted the foundry sand upwards to fall into a huge storage tank reached by a steel ladder with flimsy safety rails on top. You were expected to climb in through a round hatch, lower yourself down into the tank and shovel the sand level in order to fill it to capacity, then with luck the plant could be closed down for a while. Heaven knows what that fine sand did to our lungs. This routine nearly cost me my life, nobody had told me a sand tanker was due and I was sent into the tank to level the sand with a shovel, unbeknown to me the tanker was underneath. The driver of the vehicle released the valve to let out the flood of fine sand, I felt the flow of sand taking me down, the elevator was still running and I was being covered by more fresh sand from above. Luckily for me my legs straddled each side of a narrow steel girder in the dark preventing me falling any further, this saved my life, having no doubt I would have been suffocated. When the lorry was filled it drove away, the driver none the wiser. I climbed up through the choking sand and lay on top of the forty feet high storage tank, it took ages to get the sand out of my eyes, chest and nose, then for my nerves to calm down. Another guardian angel moment! Certainly I had good reason to hate that drying plant with a passion, enjoying showing new starters how to run it before they too would never turn up for work.

A lucky day had seven men working, one on the sand/gravel plant, one for the sand dryer, loading shovel driver, two drivers for the tractor trailers running in tandem from the lagoons bringing spoil to the plants, dragline operator and our foreman. We have worked with just me and the foreman occasionally, he drove the tractor trailer down to the dragline loaded and bought a load to the dryer hopper for me to run through. Meanwhile if a lorry called for a load of gravel I operated the loading shovel, which is why we got on so well, we carried on working the quarry if nobody else turned up. In return I got free fuel and oil for my boat enjoying every minute it was nearly as good as fishing. When the foreman had to report to the office in Barrow, he left me in charge which being a teenager was a nice feeling. In a year I had learned to drive all the vehicles, fix all the plant and learned skills that came in useful for the rest of my life. The fact that health and safety did not exist did not bother me unduly, I just took life as it came, when our tractors had no brakes due to sand wearing out brake pads and the handbrakes did not work, you stopped the vehicles by stalling them then leaving them in gear!

The time had come to go full time fishing, my new trawl nets were paid for and new echo sounder fitted in the boat. Mother's outstanding bills were paid, modern windows, a new bathroom and furniture bought. The entire house had been modernised, only me at home now my siblings were all married. Sadly I said good bye to my friend the foreman I would miss him a lot, his parting words were "You are welcome back anytime Norm!"

My wish was to catch enough fish to buy a bigger boat if successful in my new venture, at least I had avoided any loans up to date and every possession of mine was paid for. Looking back with hind sight maybe I should have just gone to the bank like most fishermen and borrowed a huge amount for a new trawler, instead of buying for cash the fishermen's old cast off boats, then spending most of my time repairing them. I suppose growing up under my mother's influence answers that question, any debt worried me. With Barrow not being a commercial fishing harbour like Fleetwood or Hull and me having no professional background or experience, any bank would refuse me a loan anyway. Leaving school with no formal qualifications, I was good at art and rugby league. When attending interviews for jobs, I said give me a trial for a week with no pay and if you are not happy with my work I will walk away, it usually worked! My assets were nil except for my boat worth about five hundred pounds now she was done up. At least if I could not make wages for two men the boat could be tied up and we could get a job then save up again.

CHAPTER TWELVE

Eighteen years old and finally I became a skipper owner, full time fisherman my own boss, sinking or swimming was now down to me literally. My dream of fishing a prawner full time after meeting those Fleetwood fishermen when I was a school kid was about to come true.

My best friend still had a couple of years to finish his apprenticeship so I found a deck hand to crew for me. One lovely spring sunny morning saw the Misty Morn heading past a new build submarine on Vickers slips, gliding past on the ebb tide full of excitement for the future, some of the men giving us a cheery wave. After reaching Lightning Knoll buoy we steamed twenty minutes past to avoid the rough ground, shot the trawl and towed westerly for two hours excited to see what might come up in the cod end, plotting on my chart the approximate position each tow. We navigated with a chart, watch and compass, no radio transmitter or GPS in those days for small boats, just using marks ashore or dead reckoning. After a few hauls I planned to land my first catch in Fleetwood, sign on with an agent who would take out our expenses, fuel etc. and give us our share left at the end of the week. Landing fresh fish daily should fetch decent prices, but like all fishermen you learn quickly the agents always find clever excuses for giving you piss poor prices. One young fish agent drove a Rolls Royce that about summed it up.

The first tow the boat pulled up dead, propeller threshing the water, the warps coming together told me that we had a hum dinger of a fastener. Two hours later we had got the warps in, the two otter boards aboard and a strop put around the cod end. Our boat was on her beam ends with the heavy weight, the lifting derrick was making horrible cracking noises with the strain. Finally getting it aboard we saw it was a huge round boulder with white painted words saying "From Bear Island" some deep sea trawler man's idea of a joke! The sweat was pouring off us so we did not see the funny side of his sense of humour. This huge boulder had crushed six large lobsters and some prime fish to pulp. All this bother was costing us money in lost fishing time. We steamed slowly back towards Lightning Knoll in calm conditions to dump the boulder onto the rough ground to avoid another small boat catching it in their trawl. I was not feeling so good after all that pulling and riving needing more pain killers to help me to carry on. The next two tows we were pleased with so set a course for Fleetwood to land our maiden catch.

We sailed into Fleetwood channel in the company of several prawners and keel boats with names such as Judy, Annie, Harriet, Biddy, Northfleet, Reynard all heading in on the early flood tide to land their catch. All the fishing boats had a flock of gulls around them wheeling and diving for bits as the crews gutted the last fish. On the horizon came into view the unmistakable silhouettes of the deep sea trawlers on their way back from faraway Iceland, Greenland and Bear Island loaded with cod, hake, and halibut after trips of three week duration. We took our turn to squeeze into a small corner of Jubilee quay and placed our tally's with our boat's name printed, onto the top layer of fish in each box to be delivered to Ernie Salthouse the fish salesman I had chosen. The larger trawlers landed into the dock where the fuel and ice facilities were. Our catch was four boxes of small plaice, one box of large plaice, two boxes of skate, and the icing on the cake two stone of dover sole a high value fish. Our fish were sold, expenses deducted and our first wage was burning a hole in our pockets. We worked on a share system one share for the boat and one each for us after the expenses were taken out. Time for a shower and bacon butty at the Seaman's Mission, a fantastic organisation a god send to sailors up and down the country, a clean friendly place to visit away from home with a warm welcome.

Fleetwood was a bustling port in those days the pubs always full of fishermen either just landed or on their way, having a last drink. Hundreds of boats of all shapes and sizes waiting on the tide to sail, the famous deep water trawlers such as Armana, Boston Blenheim, Wyre Revenge, Samuel Hewett, Josena, Ssafa, Ella Hewett, all consigned to history now. Once part of a proud British fleet of highly skilled men who risked their lives to bring us our fish and too often paid the ultimate price! Now a walk around those same docks is a sad walk for me, only three small trawlers still fishing and the huge dock converted into a marina. Houses have been built where the fish merchants traded, I suppose it is progress but the heart has gone out of the place.

Later that night having a few pints in the Fleetwood Arm's, I was chatted up by a bonnie looking girl called Gloria who told me she had been discharged from the army for medical reasons. One drink led to another and Gloria suggested I take her to a newly opened posh Chinese restaurant, I had never been out for a meal before certainly not with a beautiful lady on my arm, excited and a little drunk we set off.

The Chinese was very posh a doorman opened the door for us and a waitress took our jackets to hang up. I let Gloria pick the meal as I did not have a clue also she ordered a carafe of house wine and a pint for me.

Looking around I saw the place was packed out we must have got the last table available, when I looked back Gloria was ordering another carafe of wine, the first one had gone already. During our starter I had a chance to look at my companion thinking she was about five years older than me, and very pretty, she must have thought me very inexperienced.

"This wine is excellent Norm you won't mind if I order another?" I was still drinking my first pint!

This was way out of my comfort zone, suddenly she rolled up her sleeves to show some tattoo's, proudly she said "This one is my regimental crest, this one say's (No gut's no glory) the other ones I can show you later!" and gave me a big wink!

I asked Gloria what her job was in the army.

"A clerk in the personnel office, a good way to get plenty of dates, it was a fantastic life Norm!"

The level of wine dropped and her voice got louder, I was very concerned about spending every penny I had earned off my first fish landing, this date was not going to plan at all. Our main course arrived Gloria ordered another carafe then started to tell me a story in a very loud voice that made all the surrounding diners and the waiter's ears prick up.

"A date every night Norm the soldiers were fighting over me, I was even smuggled into their barracks one night, I thought I had died and gone to heaven!"

"Lost count of the soldiers I slept with, still write to some of them!"

Suddenly Gloria did not seem so attractive and neither did the thought of my bill at the end of the night.

"How many women have you slept with Norm?" she said so that everyone in the restaurant overheard her.

My face felt hot and I knew I was blushing, in a low voice I told her that I had not slept with any woman yet.

"You are fucking kidding me, you're still a virgin?" she shouted at the top of her voice!

The diners stopped eating the waiters stopped waiting everyone was focused on what Gloria would say next. Suddenly you could have heard a pin drop.

"Tonight's the night Norm, your boat has just come in I am going to give you the time of your life!"

Gloria waved the waiter over and said "Bring me a bottle of your best wine, none of that cheap shite you have been serving me with all night, we are celebrating!"

"No offence Gloria it sounds like you have slept with half the British army no wonder you had to leave on medical grounds!" I said in a low voice. "Your tattoo should say I am just a girl who can't say no!"

Now that was a big mistake!

"Are you calling me a slag? You cheeky little prick!"

She stood up then upended my dinner plate and contents on top of my head. Gloria grabbed the bottle of wine off the table and strode towards the exit pushing an unfortunate Chinese waiter onto the lap of a surprised diner saying "What the fuck are you staring at?"

The place was in an uproar, most of the diners were splitting their sides with laughter, only the odd ones showed me a little sympathy as I sat with chicken chow mien running down my face and neck. Four waiters stood at the exit to prevent me doing a runner. Mustering all my remaining dignity I shoved all my money into the hand of the girl at the till, hoping it would be enough. Walking down the high street I could still hear the laughter that Gloria's cabaret provoked. Gloomily climbing into the cabin back at the boat my mate said "Had a good night Norm?"

"I would rather not talk about it!" I said.

Next morning I was picking rice out of my hair and nursing a really bad head having had little sleep. The quay was bustling with fishermen carrying their bag of sandwiches for the day. Most of our little boats fished only a tide each day. The air was thick with exhaust fumes from all the cold engines starting up. Navigation lights came on and after a quick fag and coffee we all started to cast off heading across Tiger's Tail bank. Steaming on the ebb tide down Wyre channel, an armada of boats all splitting up at the mouth of the channel to head for each skipper's favourite fishing tows. My choice was a day trawling off Blackpool for plaice as the prices were good, trying to recoup my losses from Gloria's unforgettable night out. That's a tale I would not be repeating to anybody for a very long time!

After a few weeks working from Fleetwood my crew decided to pack in fishing. He rightly could not stand the primitive conditions of living on my small boat any longer, so we took Misty Morn back to Barrow, my crew soon got a proper job as he called it! The time had come to buy a bigger boat with a roomier cabin for living aboard, back to saving up again with a high paying job. By this time all my siblings had long gone so our house was quiet and peaceful at last, I appreciated a room and my own bed after all those years of sharing, what bliss! About this time I helped dad to buy the house to save paying out rent each week and helped to modernise it.

Cycling up the road to the North Walney quarry I felt a bit cheeky going to ask the foreman if there were any vacancies, I need not have worried they were short handed as usual, having a large rush order on for dried sand. At going home time I was offered my old job back coming in early in the morning just like old times. Seemingly the man who took over from me could not stand it any longer! I thought it pays to give your job one hundred percent and to leave on good terms!

After working at the quarry for a week or so I was phoned by a friend from the sailing club to give me the bad news that my lovely Misty Morn had sunk on the mooring. It was a Sunday morning so that at least meant plenty of bodies available to help me, I hoped. Getting a lift down to Ferry beach I stepped out of the car and wondered where all these people had come from, some were carrying coils of rope, someone had bought flasks of tea and sandwiches. Many new faces were from other sailing clubs in the area all saying they wanted to help in any way they could. At low tide we managed to get a pump aboard and soon had her pumped out. Laying out a long warp to pull her up the beach on the flood tide.

It touched me that so many people turned up to help. I really do not think the same reaction would occur nowadays, hoping I am wrong! The problem was the friend's mooring I had left her on, the onshore wind had blown her bow up the steep bank leaving her counter in the gulley, she did not have the lift on the flood tide so the cockpit filled up, it had turned out a bad choice of mooring. We worked my boat up the beach to safety then set to and ate all the sandwiches, sharing out the tea donated by so many people. I had a tear in my eye saying goodbye to everyone that night I would never forget their kindness to a teenage lad who would be eternally grateful! We worked all night cleaning out the mud from inside the hull and flushed out the engine. I luckily had a spare starter motor also managing to borrowed another battery and alternator, she was fired up again and ran sweetly. This was all thanks to my gifted engineer and best friend Brian who never let me down. Not many people had their boats insured or could afford to, so thanks to our friends in the boating community we lived to fight another day. Norm could easily have ended up with nothing to show for all the years of scrimping and saving! My friend and I made it to work as usual having had no sleep all night but I could not have been happier. When a fellow boater was in trouble then we all rallied round and helped each other, good days, and a great close knit community.

One of the last fishing trips I had with the Misty Morn was well over in Morecambe bay in a long deep channel that was left when the tide went out leaving the surrounding sand banks exposed. This channel sometimes yielded good catches that had drained off the sand leaving the fish trapped with nowhere to go until the tide flooded in again. A strange feeling towing up and down with high sand banks on either side spreading out for miles. When the wind dried the sand the bay looked like a desert. We touched on the bottom occasionally in this very shallow water but soon worked her into deeper depths again. This is the environment that the prawner was designed for, shallow waters and the short steep seas encountered here. We filled the boat with skate until we could not carry any more, when enough water entered the bay we steamed across to Fleetwood landing our bumper catch in Jubilee quay.

To celebrate our good fortune we went out for a few pints around Fleetwood, my crew got fixed up with a girl saying he would meet up with me on the boat later. Stood at the bar on my own I noticed the pretty barmaid smiling at me, we got chatting I asked her if she would mind me walking her home when the pub closed. After she gave it some thought I was pleased when she said yes. Making myself useful I collected empty glasses and emptied the ash trays around the pub. Chatting as she cashed up behind the bar she said her name was Jane, was divorced from a violent husband and had three young children to bring up. Jane was blond, blue eyed and beautiful, about ten years older than me. We left the pub and walked through the dark, drizzly streets, holding hands and stopping frequently to give each other lingering kisses. Blimey this is romantic she was a little smasher, lucky me. Jane lived in a row of tiny terraced houses near the fish dock not unlike my house in Glasgow Street.

At her front door I kissed her and thanked her for a lovely night turning around to go, after all it was late. She seemed a trifle surprised when I turned to leave "Don't you want to come in for a night cap Norm?" I did not need to be asked twice, kicking off my shoes I walked into the lounge surprised to see her kids still up watching television, but it was a Saturday night. Jane introduced me to the kids and poured us both a large brandy, holding my hand she led me upstairs to bed, me thinking that I was having a good dream and shortly would wake up to find myself tucked up in my damp bunk on the Misty Morn. Her bedroom was all pink and cosy the bed looked full of promise. Jane switched on the bedside light and started to undress me. I felt myself blushing my hands began to shake as I helped her with my shirt buttons.

"This is your first time isn't it Norm?" she said.

Nodding, my mouth suddenly felt very dry, watching her slowly undressing she looked absolutely beautiful. Feeling like I had just won the football pools the moment I had been waiting for had at last arrived!

Jane told me to get into bed and as I bent down to pull back the sheet a painful back spasm made me cry out in pain.

"What is the matter?" Jane asked with concern in her voice.

"Handling a ton of fish today Jane my back is giving me grief I am so sorry about this!"

"No problem Norm" fetching a tube of 'Fiery Jack' pain reliever out of her bedside drawer proceeded to slap it all over my back, hell fire it was hot I said "Clever girl that has hit the spot!"

At last this is what I have waited for to happen for a long time, my prayer has been answered! Feeling like the cat that got the cream I climbed into her bed.

They say that all good things come to an end, well mine never started! She grabbed my manhood in both hands I felt the greatest pain ever experienced, it was like having thousands of red hot needles stabbing into my willy! I must have jumped three feet in the air and then done a war dance around her bedroom. In the moment of passion Jane had neglected to wash the 'Fiery Jack' off her hands!

"The pain, the pain, bloody hell!" I shouted in desperation.

Jane told me to quickly wash my privates in cold water in her bathroom. The bathroom she informed me was downstairs and to go through the lounge to reach it. By this time the pain was nigh on unbearable I dashed downstairs (naked except for a pillow placed strategically over my bits) passing the children still watching television shouting that "I was very sorry it was an emergency!" Dipping my crown jewels in very cold water in the bathroom I could hear the children's hysterical laughter in the lounge. I only hoped that I had not done permanent damage, it took two hours for the pain to subside, when I finally limped back up to the bedroom Jane was snoring away and her kids were in bed. Putting my clothes back on I quietly let myself out of the house limping back to my boat through the deserted streets. My pride was hurt I was feeling sorry for myself and took pains to avoid the pub where Jane worked for a long time! This was another incident that I was keeping to myself for the foreseeable future. My efforts with the opposite sex scored a great big zero. My mate commented for a while after how my limp seemed to be getting worse maybe I should see a doctor.

CHAPTER THIRTEEN

Misty Morn was sold to a man who lived in Fleetwood. Delivering her across the bay we were caught in a hum dinger of a violent gale. The new owner was amazed when he saw us steaming up the Wyre channel, a tribute to the prawner's sea going abilities. The hunt was on for another boat with more accommodation and a fish room, so I could do longer trips. The prawner's were designed for tidal work and unsuitable to live on. My friend had converted his Commer van into a motor home he volunteered to drive us up the east coast of Scotland to Wick, then down the west side looking into every small harbour on our quest for my perfect little trawler. Every little creek was explored and every harbour side pub was investigated, most still had a small prosperous fleet of small boats crabbing or lobstering, managing to keep their way of life intact.

Many years later I hired a motor home and did the same trip, I could have wept. The lovely traditional wooden boats had gone the harbours were full of plastic yachts. Most of the pretty harbour side fishermen's cottages were now holiday homes, the heart had gone out of the place. At least I had the privilege to have seen the traditional working fishing harbours that are now few and far between.

The best way to find out what is for sale is to visit the harbour side pub, we found the land lord would always invite you to park up there for the night and usually put a cooked breakfast on. Stonehaven, Pittenweem, Peterhead all had boat's for sale, the old story too expensive, they were making good money then, the only way would be a large bank loan. It was not as if my money was not building up, always making a good profit when selling my boat after all the hours of work going into them. I grafted at work doing loads of overtime. Still I was only eighteen and optimistic that my dream boat would turn up sometime. One night sitting with a group of fishermen in a pub at Aberdeen one happened to tell a tale about a wooden fifty footer lying at Oban on the west coast, she only needing some engine repairs. Pausing only long enough to thank him for the information we jumped into the van and drove overnight from the east coast to the west pulling into beautiful Oban, the gateway to the isles!

There was a large fleet in Oban some catching prawns and lots of visiting boats landing scallops, enquiring where our boat was we saw that she was moored off the island of Kerrera, straight across the sound from Oban. We wondered how to get to her we needed some kind of boat. My mate pointed to a row of varnished rowing boats for hire pulled up on the beach in front of us. "Simple our problem is solved! We can hire a rowing boat row across the sound and look around the boat at our leisure if we find it suitable then we can contact the owner!"

The dour looking boat hirer complete with tartan kilt took our money and pushed us out pointing to a big orange marker buoy about one hundred yards out, "Do not go passed the buoy!" We rowed straight passed the orange buoy and I felt uncomfortable about what we had decided to do, the man was waving his fist and shouting at us.

"Don't worry! We will give him a big tip when we get back Norm so stop worrying" said my pal. The trawler was Norwegian style with a lovely varnished hull and wheelhouse she was built like a battleship. Slowly we rowed around her admiring her graceful lines. It had been a long row across a lot further than it looked. We were a bit knackered forgetting all about our irate boat hirer back in Oban. We climbed aboard feeling very excited that this boat may soon belong to me! The boat was perfect except that the engine was in huge bits in the engine room and looked very old, we realised the parts would be very expensive so reluctantly decided not to pursue it further.

Despondent we climbed into our rowing boat and slowly started to head towards Oban to face the music, me thinking that the hirer might have reported us to the police for stealing his boat. The wind had got much stronger by this time the waves were getting higher. We were not too concerned after all our rowing boat was seaworthy. All the years rowing in the tide races of Walney channel made these conditions seem a piece of cake. Mind you I must concede it looked bad with having no life jackets or anchor in the boat. To make matters worse a bloody great Calmac car ferry was hooting his foghorn at us. The captain came out of the bridge to wave his fist. This had not been such a good idea we seemed to have pissed off a lot of people in a short time.

"He is certainly pissed off Norm!" Brian said pointing shore wards where an irate man in a kilt was jumping up and down waving a fist in the air and shouting!

"There seems to be a large crowd of onlookers waiting to see what all the excitement is about" I said.

We pulled into the beach and the predominate words we could make out were "You fucking Sassenach bastards!"

I knew he would be a little bit annoyed but when offered a fistful of cash he angrily knocked it out of my hands into the water.

After all we had returned his boat intact, but it looked like he was going to have a heart attack or hit me. My friend said "Run like fuck Norm!" Many years after I was aboard a Calmac ferry on the way to Mull and was invited onto the bridge by the captain. Having a yarn I mentioned that the rowing boats were not at Oban anymore and wondered about the man in the kilt that hired them out? "That was a relative of my friend he often told us a tale about two young English boys who pinched his boat. They rowed to Kerrera to look at a fishing boat, on the way back they held up a car ferry then were caught in a gale of wind. He said they were bloody nutter's but by hell they knew how to handle a set of oars. We always wondered what became of the two boys"

After all the miles travelling around Scotland I saw an advert in the Fishing News paper for bids to be left at Ramster's fish agents at Fleetwood, for a bonnie little fishing smack named 'Fruitful'.

She was lying in Jubilee quay, going aboard her we saw that the Kelvin J3 diesel engine was in bits spread around the fish room.

The moment I saw Fruitful I wanted her with a passion, so dashed around to the agent's office to have a word.

"Have you had any offers?" I asked.

"One thousand five hundred is what we are expecting for her she is quite a newish boat and only needs spare parts to get her back to sea, what are you offering Mister Pascoe?"

My total amount of cash was nine hundred and fifty pounds after bailing out my mother yet again, paying all the final demands accumulating in the usual place behind the clock on the mantel piece. The agent laughed at my offer, but I made him write down my telephone number just in case a miracle happened! Two weeks later I had a call from Fruitful's agent offering me the boat at my price, I was over the moon! It cleaned me out financially and I would have to start saving for the expensive engine parts plus all the other gear needed for a new boat.

A couple of weeks later saw the Fruitful being towed across Morecambe bay by my friend's boat 'Sea Witch' named after his mother in law. We all had sore heads after celebrating all night in the Fleetwood Arms. We took out the Kelvin engine taking it to our boat shed for a complete overhaul. I bought all the expensive parts when I had saved enough money. The Fruitful was built in 1955 at Millers of St. Monans and registered as KY40, when I fished her it was FD10. In her small cabin we had two bunks, cooker, coal stove, mid ships was a fish room, aft was engine room where lived a Kelvin J3 petrol / diesel hand start. The engine on rare occasions was a bitch to start if the magneto was damp. A sentry box type wheelhouse was aft and in front of the wheelhouse was a set of capstan barrels for winching in the trawl warps, a similar way to hauling on a prawner. No toilet was fitted so still bucket and chuck it! The ritual for starting the Kelvin was to pray hard then start to swing the starting handle, starting it on petrol then when warm switch over to diesel. Snag was there was not a lot of head room in the engine room compartment to swing a starting handle meaning always having skinned knuckles and lower back pain! Once my friend had over hauled the engine a new depth finder was installed, we were then ready to earn money with our boat.

We made and laid several yacht moorings in Walney channel also down at Piel Island which made me solvent once more. Several fishing parties were taken out after I had obtained a local boatman's licence for twelve anglers, which we took out most weekends. Strangely it was the head of the council bus depot who came down to test me for a Boatman's licence which legally entitled the carrying of twelve passengers, also checking my safety gear flares, lifejackets and so on. Then I had to take him for a trip down channel to check out the engine, unfortunately for me when in the most congested part of Walney channel, in a racing tide rip the idiot shouted to me to do an emergency stop as if I was driving in a car on the high street in town. If I had attempted to go astern the tide would have swept me onto the many moored yachts and caused carnage. He was well put out when I told him what I thought of his brain wave. To his credit he passed me for a licence saying I was the youngest licence holder in the area he would be keeping his eye on me. In later years of course it became a lot harder to pass the test and more official departments became involved, including the police.

The Fruitful was thirty two feet in length drawing three and half feet draught, so I had to be careful not to run aground fishing in my favourite shallow channels in Morecambe bay. The full keel made Fruitful very hard to keep in the narrow twisting channels of the bay but I took the chance because of the consistently good catches of plaice and skate. The downside was being trapped far up the bay when the weather deteriorated, leaving us trapped in a channel or large pool having to wait until the tide had come in to allow us to sail out with a safe depth of water under us. By this time we would receive a right pasting and it did not do my nerves much good, but if we waited for a perfect forecast we would never sail or ever make any money.

Sometimes trapped in our secret channels well up the bay towards Ulverston channel, we could hear the shrimpers in their tractors towing behind them a trailer with shrimp net attached. They were fishing the shallow channels for the famous Morecambe bay brown shrimps. These brown shrimp are picked, potted in butter the small tubs are even sold in Harrods, they taste like food of the Gods, if you have not tried them you are missing out! The tractor fishermen must have been surprised to see two ships mast sticking up above the sand banks in the middle of Morecambe bay as we towed slowly up and down. A week or two later the channels and pools could move again meaning you would have to find them again.

Occasionally when off the shores of Walney Island dolphins and porpoise would give us a wonderful show of acrobatics. The first time I saw a basking shark feeding was a sight I will never forget. We were drifting on a calm sea using feathers to hook mackerel when this huge black shape swam past our boat with two dorsal fins protruding out of the water. Our boat was ten metres in length this basking shark was slightly longer.

Afterwards the fishery officer said it must have been all of seven tons being that length, to think they bulk up eating plankton! Just after the war these beautiful creatures were nearly hunted to extinction in the Western Isles of Scotland for their huge livers, the rest of the carcass dumped in deep water. They were killed by harpoons even some Norwegian boats came to Scotland for the fishery. Now they are fully protected thank goodness.

Westminster dredging who had the contract for deepening Walney channel for the next launch asked us if we would like to hire out the Fruitful. They wanted to use our boat acting as supply tender for several weeks to the dredger this meant giving up my quarry job once again. This time it was forever as another firm had just taken over, it was nice while it lasted. After working twenty four hours a day tendering to the trailer suction dredger I was tired. This dredging method was to move up and down the channel dragging a long pipe with a drag head on the seabed, working the same as a household hoover, it sucked up the mud and when loaded the dredger headed out to the dumping grounds to empty her load of spoil. I was glad when the contract finished and could return to fishing.

That summer was a good year in Morecambe bay for tiny seed mussel they covered a large area of sand flats. The flounders found the seed beds and went mad gorging on it, when you gutted them they were bursting with these tiny mussels. Some days the water was clear as gin, looking over the bow into the six or eight feet of water we were trawling in, you could see the large flounder swimming about below. This was similar to looking into a giant aquarium. We had only two or three feet of water under our keel the bright orange net floats were on the surface, clouds of sand was kicking up behind us, we knew we were going to have a large catch of flounders. The first haul the flounders were stacked into the net like slates, it took several lifts to empty the net they filled the fish room from top to bottom. The next haul filled the fish pounds overflowing onto the deck. We had every seagull from miles around in a feeding frenzy diving and squabbling for the guts. That day we must have gutted thousands of fish until our fingers were sore, then called it a day heading out of the bay back to Barrow instead of Fleetwood. The Fruitful was deep in the water, sluggish with the weight of flatties aboard. The prices were better selling to a local lad who bagged them up five for fifty pence taking them to pubs as far as Kendal in the Lake District. We landed them into his van and one ton trailer, which to our surprise held a large quantity of south end of Walney rabbits, I wonder who shot those?

The price for flounder (flukes) was never good over the years sometimes not even worth landing in quantity, but a lot better nowadays when you can get good prices off shellfish fishermen who are using them for pot bait. Species like flukes, dabs, gurnards, and mullet are appreciated these days thanks to television and the celebrity chefs. They have shown the public the right way to prepare and cook these fish to show off their wonderful different taste, well done them! Getting back to my tale the next day he told me that everything sold like hotcakes and to keep fetching in the flukes. Eventually our friend's customers were ready for a change so we had to leave the shallow mussel beds and move offshore to find higher value species of fish. One of the good things about fishing and self employment is the freedom to change tack and use the boat for different types of work that sometimes became available.

CHAPTER FOURTEEN

We were scrubbing the weed and barnacles off the Fruitful's hull, it was before the days of power washers and we were knackered. A voice shouted off the quayside "Got an interesting job for you Norm!" It was our friend Peter who happened to be a shipping agent. Over a brew he told us about our new charter, it was to salvage a large nearly new fishing boat that had sunk off Halfway shoal. This was very near the main channel leading into the port of Barrow. The salvage company who had the original contract had failed for a variety of reasons, and now the port authority needed it shifting soon as possible. Explosives could not be used because of the proximity of the dredged main channel used for submarines. The downside to this salvage was the exposed position the trawler was lying in, on a corner almost continuously swept by heavy seas and strong tidal currents. She was partly showing at low water on a spring tide a real danger to other vessels running into her.

The trawler was called 'Stephil' and registered A41 which was Aberdeen, a nearly new boat built by the Thorne shipyard of Richard Dunston. She was seventy three feet in length and powered by a Lister Blackstone diesel. Stephil was built for near water fishing was one of the one hundred and eight near, middle and distant water vessels fishing out of Fleetwood. She was the third new trawler to enter service at Fleetwood that year in 1968, all near water vessels. Stephil was a fine built ship with a twenty foot beam and ten feet draught. Every modern safety aid the wheelhouse full of the latest electronics. The story we heard was she developed engine problems off the coast of Walney in a terrible gale and the ship was abandoned, the crew taken off safely by a trawler called the Craigmillar. Stephil eventually washed ashore near Walney lighthouse and the next tides made higher than predicted washing her back out to sea, some hatches were not secured and in stormy seas she filled up and sank near the dredged channel. The harbour authority put down a green wreck buoy to mark her position.

We were hired by a famous company called United Towing of Hull to take divers and salvage equipment out to the wreck. At nineteen years of age it was very exciting for me and a dream fulfilled. Our first task was to take out divers to do a complete up to date survey of the wreck then report the findings to the newly appointed salvage master Captain.

This seaman was very experienced and had worked all over the world on major shipwrecks. We anchored over the wreck on a lovely rare calm day, and the divers began their survey of the hull's condition for the salvage master to decide the best way to begin the recovery. We returned at low water and saw that parts of the wreck were showing above water, the top of the wheelhouse, whaleback and a gallows which was handy for us to tie heavy mooring ropes on, to save time when mooring up. Ropes and lengths of trawl netting were caught around railings and mast that needed to be removed first. The previous salvagers had cut down her main mast, the ship's wheel, compass, bell and lights had been removed for souvenirs. The divers did not have a long working time on the wreck during spring tides as the tide ran so strongly. We had to use all our strength to pull them back to our ship using their air hose. We acted as linesmen to the two divers once we had our boat moored up safely and looked after the compressor, hoses etc.

The divers and salvage master stayed in a lovely hotel at Rampside. We lived on the Fruitful moored at Roa Island near the lifeboat station, rowing ashore each tide to pick them up at the jetty along with our hotel packed sandwiches for the day. Luckily we had a spell of settled weather to start with and the divers could start clearing all the loose debris from around the wreck. Trawl nets wrapped around everywhere had to be cut free and loose ropes that could snag up a diver. All the many aluminium fish pound boards from the large fish room had to be pulled aboard Fruitful. We were kept supplied with lobster and crab by the divers as they delved deeper into the wreck so we all ate well! The plan was to clear the Stephil of all loose items and then have made to measure strong patches put over all the hatches, windows and portholes. All the patches were fitted with connections so that compressed air could be blown into the ship. In theory the wreck would come to the surface and we could tow her into Barrow harbour. Well that was the master plan we could not wait for that moment to arrive. A large heavy duty diesel suction pump was delivered from Hull on the east coast, the divers started to pump out the silt washed into the ship by the winter storms. It must have been very difficult for the divers to get into all the nooks and crannies, we could see a long trail of black mud drifting down tide showing what a good job they were doing. The diver emergency signal for us to pull them up was three sharp tugs on their lifeline. This happened one day whilst they were working in the fish room. Pulling up the diver quickly and dragging him aboard, pulling off his mask we could see his eyes bulging with shock and fear. "Bloody hell I have just been attacked by a monster conger eel that I did not see at the back of the fish room in the murk, the shock nearly made me pass out I can tell you!"

His buddy that had just come to the surface said he was right about the size it was enormous and the teeth looked vicious. Somehow the monster eel needed to be killed and removed from the fish room. We packed it in for the day and headed home wondering what they were going to do to solve the conger problem. Rather them than me entering that dark space not knowing exactly where the bad tempered conger was lurking!

The next few days were very stormy the salvage team went home to collect some more equipment. We kicked our heels aboard the Fruitful playing cards in the cabin waiting for a break in the weather. The weather improved at last the divers went over the side into the wreck saying they were going to sort out the conger in the fish hold once and for all. Three tugs each and up they came onto the deck smiling about something. The salvage master asked what was going on and the divers looked at their watches and said "About now!" A muffled Crump! And a big air bubble broke the surface. Our poor boat lifted three feet out of the water and we all lost our footing and landed in a heap on the deck. "Bloody glad we did not use any more explosive we might have all ended up swimming to shore!" the senior diver said laughing.

"Well that should have put paid to master conger eel!" he said laughing.

Over the side they went again taking a rope down with them, a tug on the rope and it felt like pulling up a dead body. The eel was enormous about seven feet long and the girth of a man, still looking scary in death.

The lifting derrick was used to heave it aboard. Later on that day we passed it onto a local fishing boat to land in Fleetwood to get rid of it. When sold it paid for a night in the pub off the proceeds. Routine was restored at last the time had come to start the final salvage operation to pump air into her, bringing Stephil finally to the surface! The size and weight of the compressor needed for the salvage attempt was too big for Fruitful to safely carry.

We decided to hire a barge from Vickers to fit all the equipment on so we could tow it out to the wreck site each day. The barge was secured above the wreck and the divers had all the hoses coupled up for our first attempt to fill her with compressed air. After a while huge air bubbles broke the surface it was obvious we had a leak in a hatch somewhere and it needed attention. Typically the wind started to increase, the waves rose higher we had to recall the divers quickly. The barge started to be swept by waves not having a lot of freeboard with all the heavy equipment piled onboard. The young diver and I became marooned on the barge when the mooring ropes broke in the heavy swell. We quickly started to drift out to sea. The lads on the Fruitful were trying to untangle all the ropes and hoses they had to disconnect from the wreck as quickly as possible so could not help us for a while after we broke adrift.

We were on our own for a time drifting on the ebb tide out to sea. The wind was screaming we were both soaked with the waves and spray washing across the barge. It was dusk, wintertime, and bloody freezing, the diver still had his suit on so it was not too bad for him. He sheltered behind the still warm compressor and started to have a full panic attack. I tried to tell him that the Fruitful would be back for us soon, so calm down. The Fruitful only just managed to find us before it was pitch black, the waves were then very high threatening to wash all our gear and us overboard. We managed to pass a tow line across then began the long slow haul home against the outgoing tide. We started up the compressor so we could stand near the exhaust pipe otherwise we would have been even more frozen, I gave the world record prize for the greatest whiner to my young diver friend. Tied up safely at Roa Island we dropped off the salvage team hoping that tomorrow the weather would be suitable for another final salvage attempt.

There were three of us on board Fruitful now we needed an extra pair of hands to be onboard Stephil for the tow into Barrow, when we had her once more floating again. Our small cabin was getting rather cramped.

The dark winter nights seemed long playing card games with only a radio to listen to. The next day after dropping off the salvage team late afternoon, we decided to take the divers large fast inflatable boat ashore to have a few rums to warm us up in the Ship Inn on Piel Island.

The wind was strong, snow showers were leaving a covering of white over everything and it was freezing cold. We all jumped ashore at the ferry landing and the young lad said he would tie up the inflatable while we got the rums in. We were made very welcome by the inn's landlord he was on his own not having had any visitors for a few days. He seemed very glad of our company it must have been very lonely on the island. We all sat by a roaring log fire supping our rums feeling all right with the world thawing out nicely. Somebody commented that our deck hand was taking his time and maybe we should see what the delay was. We all piled outside in the gathering dusk to look for him, seeing the dinghy was not tied to the jetty and no sign of him. This was very strange we walked down towards the jetty then spotted his footprints in the snow coming towards the pub. At the high water mark a pile of his clothes were discarded. Then we saw his footprints going back towards the jetty, on which stood his boots. Looking seawards between the crest of the waves we could make out the divers black inflatable drifting out to sea and in the gloom could just make out a white torso trying to climb aboard.

"Jesus the mad bastard swam all that way in this weather he should be dead with hyperthermia by now, the bloody idiot it was not worth risking his life for!" I said. The engine roared into life and he headed back at full speed ramming the boat straight up the beach. We carried his blue body up to the pub putting him in warm blankets, giving him a few hot rum toddies to revive him. Eventually when his teeth stopped chattering he told us what had happened. He had tied the dinghy up wrongly, he turned around to check, only to see it drifting away on the ebb tide he was frightened of what the senior diver would say or do to him. This diver was a giant bad tempered man and built like a brick shithouse, I could see the lads point if it had been me I probably would have done the same! His youth and fitness saved him he was a lucky young man, also lucky on a future occasion.

The next morning we were called to a meeting at the salvage team's hotel. The forecast was still foul and the Barrow harbour master informed us that a submarine was leaving Barrow very shortly so we had run out of time. The salvage master and diving team were gutted, we were so near succeeding all our work was to no avail. The good news was that we found out Europe's biggest floating crane was passing in the Irish Sea after successfully salvaging a coaster off the rocks in Southern Ireland, how lucky was that! A call to the insurance company paying the bill and a fair price was agreed with Taklift 2 to start the salvage of Stephil the next day.

We dropped off the barge at Vickers shipyard and unloaded all the salvage equipment at Ferry beach, typically the weather calmed down meaning we could have had our final attempt to blow air into her, it was not to be. Our last job on hire to Hull Towing was to assist the Taklift 2 in any way we could with our local knowledge.

She had two large tugs assisting and her team of divers soon had heavy steel cables running underneath her hull. The captain of the crane barge asked us to go and trawl for a few boxes of fish to stock up their freezers. We were soon back with a good few boxes of plaice, in time to see Stephil come out of the water, and then lashed to the bow of the floating crane. They had several baskets of crabs and lobsters out of the Stephil the crew would dine like lords for a long time. Our reward was several bottles of best malt whisky and several cartons of duty free cigarettes. The crane barge headed for Fleetwood but realising the tide there was a bit low to enter turned back to Barrow then lifted Stephil out onto dry land to be scrapped. The insurance company offered us the Stephil in lieu of our fee for all the months hire money, after giving it a lot of thought I declined their offer. The Lister Blackstone engine and the expensive Norwinch were refurbished and sold on, the hull was scrapped.

We took some great photos of the salvage but were glad to move on, I was only twenty my own master still making a wage much to my father's surprise. He had retired from the shipyard where he worked as a crane driver and spent his evenings as a doorman at the Working Men's club in the town centre. Dad's health was not too good his heavy smoking did not help. Now the house was empty he had mellowed spending his days reading cowboy books. Mum just pottered about the house relying on my wages after I cancelled all her credit in the corner shops and gave her cash to pay. My real love was still fishing so decided to put Fruitful up for sale in the Fishing News to buy a bigger vessel for longer fishing trips. She was soon snapped up by a young man who wanted her for trawling in the Solway Firth out of a little harbour called Port William. A testament to her builder and to all her owner's careful attention, she is still fishing successfully now in the Orkney Islands on the scallop and prawn grounds.

The last trip we made in Fruitful before her leaving Barrow was over into the middle of Morecambe bay to have a last bash at the skate ground. Dropping over the trawl at high tide we towed around until we found the channel, only stopping fishing when towards low water we were in danger of running aground. The anchor was dropped to hold us in position while around us the high sand banks appeared. It was like being in a pool in the middle of a vast desert. Waiting for the flood tide we started gutting all the ten baskets of skate plus one box of plaice, surrounded by the usual screaming gulls. Normally we would creep out of the bay through a narrow channel with rocks either side leaving no error of judgement when calm, the problem was it had started to blow a full gale. When the flood tide started in earnest and we lifted out of the snug shelter below the sand banks we would be in a dangerous position. Another problem was my crew being a heavy smoker had run out of smokes, he was having nicotine withdrawal problems feeling ratty not helped by the danger we were in. Looking from the wheelhouse roof toward the entrance channel the sea was white with high combers rolling in, this meant that I could not pin point the exit channel exactly, so we would have to leave much later than I normally would. This is what happens when you fish the inside of Morecambe bay with a deep keeled boat you have to be prepared for possible dangerous consequences.

My friend was getting even worse tempered so I opened the tea caddy and rolled him some lookalike fag substitutes using tea with thin paper, and lighting one for myself. Next minute he was puffing away and certainly seemed to be in a little better disposition, as for me the smoke made me feel dizzy. The waves were coming over the bow the spume was blowing past, the anchor was beginning to drag it was time to leave. This tide was lower than the last so the depth over the rocks left us with even less water under our keel. We were both worried when I steered Fruitful towards the combers rolling towards us hoping my judgment of the channel was correct. Bang, we came off a wave and our keel came down on a rock, the whole boat shuddered, the masts were vibrating. It sounded like the coal stove had dislodged and had shot across the cabin, good job it was not lit! What with the wind screaming through the rigging it was a bit scary, my mate shot down below to see if we had been holed by the rock, his head appeared out of the fish room hatch giving me a thumbs up sign. Luckily we had not sustained any serious hull damage. We had some more nasty moments before we reached deeper water and could heave a sigh of relief. This episode made my mind up to buy a bigger boat to fish deeper water and make even longer trips. This was now the time to give trawling the shallow water of Morecambe bay a rest. Puddle trawling was not for the faint hearted and I felt that we had pushed our luck too far on too many occasions.

CHAPTER FIFTEEN

We did the same old travelling up and down the country looking at various trawlers, some were complete wrecks some too expensive. The inshore fishing industry was still doing alright so good boats would always be hard to find. On our own doorstep was a forty two foot trawler called 'Easter Morn' a similar class of boat as my Fruitful but much larger and bulkier. This boat was far deeper keeled so we could never fish in the shallow waters of Morecambe bay or the Duddon estuary. She was built in nineteen thirty four in Scotland at Reekies, she also starred in a black and white film about a feuding fishing family on the east coast. She fished most of her life out of Whitby longlining, lobstering and drifting for the bonnie shoals of herring. Easter Morn had a few owners since arriving in Barrow several years earlier and was laid up by the current owner due to a major engine break down. She berthed alongside the Ferry beach quay the owner invited two of us from the Fruitful to be equal partners in a new fishing venture. Our new friend was a very experienced merchant navy man who had years of service at sea, we were looking forward to working with him.

We all worked on the boat giving her a complete refit, installed a brand new marine diesel, new trawl nets, she looked a picture after a full repaint. The cabin was forward and had four bunks fitted, a new diesel fuelled heater was installed. The fish room was refitted using aluminium boards we salvaged from the 'Stephil' and could carry plenty of crushed ice for preserving the fish on longer trips. This engine room was roomy leaving plenty of space to work on the engine if needed. The large wheelhouse was varnished teak and came courtesy of good old Wards ship breakers, likewise the twelve man inflatable life raft stowed on the wheel house roof. A proper trawl winch using wire warps instead of rope sat in front of the wheel house, she had gallows fitted to hang the otter boards off instead of lifting them manually like before! She was a well rigged (vintage it must be said), inshore trawler we thought capable of making the three of us a steady wage.

The other full time boats working from Barrow were Easter Rose and Vertrouwen, we all landed our catches at Fleetwood. The practice at this time was to take out any lads who wanted a free trip to help with the gutting and suchlike, they might be on holiday or between jobs, we called them pleasurer's. We would give them a treat for helping, a bag of prime fish to take home, buy them to a few pints and a meal out after landing in Fleetwood. We landed some great catches of plaice being out a few days at a time, one particular trip we hit the plaice and landed forty five boxes of top class fish in the space of one tide, they sure did take some gutting.

An old fisherman said to me that we were floating slaughter houses one way of putting it I thought. Taking an extra hand was useful when we had large quantities of small plaice to get through and a new face on the deck to wind up.

After landing another good trip of plaice we were all out having a few pints in the Fleetwood Arms including our pleasurer, who I shall call 'Tom' for reasons of decorum. We were tired and just wanted a quiet night, until the local well known lady of the night took a shine to Tom, picking the weedy lad up and sitting him on her knee. This was easily accomplished as the lady weighed all of twenty stone and Tom about nine stone. Mandy was her name she was dressed in a pristine white trouser suit and was already drunk, belting out the 'Bonnie shoal of herring' song ignoring the landlady's calls "To shut the fuck up!"

Tom was smitten he kept ordering more pints of bitter to feed her insatiable appetite for alcohol. Tom's leather purse was opening and closing like a baby sparrow's beak, when last orders came she made Tom buy a bottle of rum to take out.

Outside Mandy asked "Where is your boat berthed Tom?"

"Are we not going back to your house Mandy?"

"Not fucking likely me husbands looking after the kids!"

"Our boat it is then" said Tom.

Unfortunately it was low tide and a twenty foot climb down a very oily dangerous steel ladder, then an awkward climb across five fishing boats, Easter Morn was the outside boat. She stood at the bottom of the ladder covered with a sheet of black oil over her once white trouser suit. Someone must have pumped their bilges out earlier the oily mess had covered most of the rungs. We were not that bothered but she was pissed off about it and her colourful language could be heard all over Fleetwood! She climbed over all the boats in the dark, bumping into every winch handle and the sharp corners of hatches like a bull in a china shop!

She even stopped on the deck of our poor boat to drop her trousers and relieve herself. "Fuck me this is not one of my better nights out!" she said loudly. We sat drinking mugs of coffee liberally dosed with rum in the cramped confines of our small cabin, Mandy's bulky body dominating the space. "Bloody Hell you could not swing a cat in this cabin, I am used to bigger boats than this!" she said. Tom was the only one on board who was excited, waiting in anticipation for a return on his investment, itching to knock off the cabin light! We three fishermen got into our bunks not looking forward to the next few minutes. The cabin went dark and I wished I had earplugs. It was embarrassing to be in such close proximity to the sounds of lovemaking between a weasel and a hippopotamus.

Thank goodness it had to come to an end, when after a long time of grunting and gasping Tom had finally got his money's worth. Then I assumed he would escort her safely home, but on reflection it would take some special kind of man to tell this lady what to do. Heavy footsteps padded across the cabin making the floorboards creak, she was shaking my friend saying "Your turn now!"

"No thanks I am too tired!" was his reply.

The next bunk was the same question and the same answer.

Now I was sweating she padded towards me and I could sense she was getting a little ratty, the smell of stale sweat and cheap perfume wafted over me. She asked me the same question and in a squeaky timid voice I answered "No thank you Mandy."

"For fuck sakes how the hell is a girl expected to earn a living, at least he owes me!" pointing towards Tom's bunk. "I will stop here the night, I am not climbing that bastard ladder again until tomorrow in daylight" at that she lifted little Tom out of his bunk, dumped him on the floor then climbed in herself. Her snoring was just as noisy as my brothers had been but not having the balls to ram a sweaty sock in her mouth I lay awake all night cursing, Tom would never sail with us ever again, that was certain!

The next morning bleary eyed I made coffee and bacon butties for us all. Loud farts and belching from Mandy's bunk signalled that the honey monster was about to grace us with her presence, I opened the hatches to let some fresh air into the cabin. All sat around the cabin table it felt a bit awkward, she looked even uglier and meaner in the daylight. Tom without his beer goggles on looked petrified. "This is a cracking bacon butty Norm!" Mandy said spitting crumbs into my face. What a state she looked, trouser suit smeared in oil, make up smudged all over her face. She had the cheek to say "Now you are sober boys who wants a shag first?"

Looking at the shocked expressions on our faces she then said "Half price then, I cannot be fairer than that boys!"

I looked at Tom and realised he thought his love making session was free his lower lip began to tremble a sure sign he was under stress.

"Go on Tom pay the lady and then escort her onto the quay we sail in thirty minutes!" I said.

His hand trembled as he opened his purse and took out a five pound note.

Quicker than a bolt of lightning Mandy took out Tom's last ten pound note and grabbed the fiver, knowing Tom would not dare say anything.

Poor Tom looked traumatised he started to help her across the line of fishing boats towards the ladder. Each boat had a hell of a roll on as she crossed. The local fishermen delighted that they had somebody to take the piss out of. Mandy just asked if anyone else was game for it before she climbed the ladder onto the quayside not batting an eyelid.

We had some interesting charters with the Easter Morn the Fisheries hired us to take some scientist out trawling for a few days, a charter with a Nuclear company up the coast at Windscale and even acted as a wreck for Barrow coast guards to practice shooting a rocket line over us. The Easter Morn was ideal for trips into the Irish Sea trawling for prawns known as Dublin Bay prawns, Norway lobster, Langoustines or just plain scampi. They live in burrows in muddy sea beds eight to twelve inches deep can live five to ten years, reaching fifteen years in exceptional cases. They look similar to lobsters but are slimmer orange pink in colour they can grow up to ten inches in length. They are nocturnal and hide in their burrows during the day, coming out at night to eat, feeding on small fish and worms, also to breed. Only the tail is consumed the rest is discarded overboard. The dawn and dusk hauls are the best the cod end bulging with the sheer volume of prawns caught, the smallest called nits took hours to nut (that is separate the tail from the head) the bigger ones are the most valuable. The taste of a fresh caught prawn or any sea fish is unforgettable, of course that was the perk of being able to take your pick from the haul then go below and prepare them for our next meal.

In those days the market for whole prawns was not like now, the prices were up and down like a whore's knickers. A nip off a prawn is like a stab from a needle and after hours spent clearing the deck you would be exhausted. All the deck work was done in the open in our day regardless of weather conditions. There were no shelter decks, just crew standing or sitting on a fish box for hour after hour in the rain or snow until the catch was sorted, gutted and stowed below in ice, then and only then could you get a quick kip before the next haul came aboard. This routine going on day and night until the skipper decides to go in to land the catch. You could not miss any good weather because there were always plenty of gales to keep you in harbour storm bound.

Seeing all the interference nowadays being bound in the Common Market fishery policies, all these other European countries sharing out our valuable fishing grounds after having decimated theirs, I just feel so sorry for our fishermen. All the inflated wages the men in suits in Brussels are awarding themselves and it looks like there are more fishery officers and officials than poor British fishermen. We have rules about this and that the only country abiding to the rules is ours! The only stress we had in my day was the weather, the fishermen now have to spend time form filling, worrying about what species and quantity of fish allowed onboard. Fishermen today must be amazed at the way of life we led free from all the bullshit! That is my rant for the day, I will need to lay down my medication must be wearing off!

My sister Jean used to worry about me like a mother hen, her husband worked in Saudi Arabia on an oil pipeline, every time he came home bought me a box of fifty King Edward cigars, which I developed quite a taste for. They added up between visits so that all the crew smoked them and we passed them about like sweets, the fish merchants thought we had won the football pools! My sister was concerned about me being so obsessed with fishing that I was not meeting a nice girl, so arranged a blind date for me much to my annoyance. I always tended to do what my sister asked we were very close, she was my best friend. The date's name was 'Judy' my sister suggested I take her to Blackpool for the day telling me to spoil her. Jean even told me what to wear and cut my hair for the date wanting nothing to go wrong. Jean said Judy was gorgeous and I would not regret it.

Pulling up at her address I could see it was one of the richest areas of Dalton and the cars in her drive cost more than our trawler. Judy and her parents were standing in the porch looking horror stricken at my ancient diesel land rover pickup truck. Switching the engine off to stop the blue exhaust cloud blowing over them, I could tell by the look on her parent's faces that they did not want their little princess to get aboard my vehicle. My sister was good friends with Judy's mum and dad otherwise they would have dragged her indoors straightaway and called the police.

Opening the car door for Judy, she climbed in and to her credit did not mention the stink of fish, just started to cough. This stale fishy smell was unsuccessfully trying to be masked by the six air fresheners Jean had hung in my cab, plus the copious amount of ladies perfume sprinkled everywhere, all of this was not working. Jumping in the driver's side I glanced at Judy, she smiled at me and I fell in love. She was beautiful, blond hair, blue eyes and a gorgeous pair of legs set off by a very short mini skirt. My first thought was bugger Blackpool lets drive to the nearest woods! Her mum and dad were both glaring at me and it was obvious hate at first sight. I started the engine at the tenth attempt and proceeded to wind down my window to tell them not to worry about their daughter that she would be safe with me, the bloody widow fell out onto their drive. Moving quickly I threw it into the back of the pickup, gunning the engine and driving quickly off before they dragged her back into the house.

We did not talk much on route to Blackpool mainly due to excessive engine noise, we soon had sore throats with shouting, I made a mental note to buy a new exhaust system. Glancing across at her made me think how lucky I was to get a date with this gorgeous creature and could not wait to park up at Blackpool, my ace sister had done well. What a lovely day it was in Blackpool the sun was shining the sky was blue. My sister had suggested a romantic carriage ride along the golden mile to impress Judy. As I helped her into the horse drawn carriage a gypsy lady thrust a long stemmed red rose into Judy's hand then said the outrageous price out loud so I would have to buy it or come across as a tight arse, gritting my teeth I thought romance is expensive! My friends said I had short arms and deep pockets but I was only a poor fisherman after all. Judy loved the romantic ride along the prom and then it was time for the meal in an expensive restaurant. This was number two suggestion from my sister and so far everything was going along just great. Judy picked an expensive bottle of wine even pronouncing the name sexily in French. I had a coke needing to keep a clear head I wanted our relationship to carry on after today. Judy had private schooling her parents obviously had high expectations of her. The meal was lovely the head waiter hovered over me like a fly on a dung heap until I had given him an enormous tip. Later Judy held my hand as we walked along the prom into the fun fair, I could see all the men looking at her then giving me envious looks.

Sauntering around the fairground King Edward cigar in my mouth I was at peace with the world, suddenly Judy squealed pointing to the Big Dipper roller coaster. She dragged me to the queue which is when I started to panic. Being a sufferer from vertigo the roller coaster was my idea of hell, Judy just ignored me when I told her my problem saying "A rough tough fisherman like you Norm it will be a piece of cake!"

Sitting in the carriage my knees knocking a half smoked cigar clamped firmly in my mouth, the ride attendant asked me if it was lit and I assured him it was not, it was just for steadying my nerves. Looking across at Judy's excited face noting how happy she looked I told myself to man up. Her mini skirt was riding well up her tanned thighs, which was some consolation the ride attendant was rudely staring at her legs as well! Thinking it will be my first ride and the last on a roller coaster I held onto her hand like grim death trying not show my fear too much. We set off and at first I coped alright screaming like everyone else, pretending to like it. We crawled up the highest incline and I looked down at the ant sized people far below then had a massive panic attack. Sweat poured down my face, I believed that I was going to have a heart attack and die. Speeding down the incline like a rocket, sucking hard on my cigar it ignited, I inhaled the smoke gratefully. Judy screamed, I screamed then bit through my cigar, the lit end dropped off and I could not give a fuck! All I wanted was to get off this dam ride soon as possible before I passed out, give me a gale of wind at sea any day of the week. The ride stopped in my blind panic I stood on Judy's hand to get off quicker, Judy screamed and pointed to my crutch shouting "Norm you are on fire!" So that was where the lit half of my cigar ended up, in my lap. Starting to beat out the smouldering cloth with my hands I looked around for some water, even my underpants were burning! The attendant rushed forward with a small fire extinguisher and emptied the lot into my crutch, poor Judy got caught in the cross fire and was speckled from head to toe in the white foam. The place was in an uproar. My date was going to rat shit and fast. Judy grabbed my hand, shouted thank you to the attendant then we both ran like hell onto the prom to find a public toilet where we could clean ourselves up. My date did not look good at this moment on her hand I could see the deep imprints of my nails and footprint. Asking Judy to wait while I went to assess my damage, she dropped a bombshell saying "So sorry Norm it is too stressful being around you, I do not ever want to see you again, please do not contact me, we are worlds apart and my parents would never approve of me going steady with a fisherman."

Judy headed toward the train station leaving me feeling gutted thinking what the hell is wrong with fishermen anyway?

Spotting a chemist across the road I asked for something to relieve my cigar burns. The chemist had to satisfy his curiosity asking me the reason for my charred trousers and when I told him, he and the girls behind the counter said this story had made their day. That's all right then I thought. Next stop to purchase a newspaper to hold in front of my crutch on the long walk back to the car park, thinking what an utter fiasco I have made of this date with the very desirable Judy. Our Jean could not wait to interrogate me about my date when I called to see her on my way home. All she could say at the end of my explanation of why Judy and I would not be marrying any time soon was "I am speechless Norm!"

My sister eventually succeeded with her match making, introducing me to the lovely lady I married and have been with for thirty eight years now, and that is another story!

CHAPTER SIXTEEN

The search for a bigger and better boat started after a fisherman from Fleetwood bought the Easter Morn off us for a good price. We looked at Fishing News adverts for trawlers for sale then set off travelling the United Kingdom looking at all the available boats, still not finding the one that suited us three partners at the right price we could afford. A friend had been to look at a tug for sale on the river Tyne at Newcastle he suggested we might get work in the docks at Barrow. The dock's board had just sold their two old vintage tugs to Greece. We figured that if we could buy the tug cheap we might earn enough money working in the dock to buy a decent trawler later on. It was worth a try nothing ventured, nothing gained!

We headed to Newcastle my land rover fully fuelled up with red diesel because we had a hundred gallons given and were trying to save money. Fingers crossed the Custom & Excise people did not stop us to dip our tank. The tug was berthed under the main Tyne Bridge we were a bit surprised to see she looked vintage, (correction she was vintage) a tall funnel, lovely varnished wood wheel house and chart house, antique hand operated anchor windlass on the bow. The Geordie man was anxious to show us around, the accommodation was very spacious, six bunks, a coal stove, all fitted out in teak woodwork with spacious lockers for the crew. The engine room was enormous compared to what we were used to, a massive Ruston Hornsby diesel with a huge flywheel dominated the engine room. The engine was started with compressed air and being a tug had lots of power from its five cylinders. Aft of the engine room was a proper tiled toilet compartment, no more bucket and chuckit. Next was a gear store for paint, tow ropes etc. A huge towing block hook was secured just aft of the funnel. She had a riveted black iron hull and was built like a battleship. We had good reason later on to be grateful to her builders for her heavy build. Her name was 'Argus' and last major contract was towing barges laden with sand up and down the east coast. Her main use now was to take out deep water angling parties into the North Sea. The owner seemed very keen to sell so we asked him to start the engine. A big roar, and a huge cloud of black smoke enveloped us, we all started to cough. The boat rolled from side to side until he knocked the revolutions down, the engine seemed to run smoothly after that. Before we could say this boat is not what we are after mister, the wee Geordie man had cast all the mooring ropes off, we were going on a trip down the river Tyne. We had been kidnapped! Standing in the wheelhouse the owner pushed my mate Stewart to the helm saying "You take the wheel canny lad while I make us all a nice brew!"

We three had a chat deciding that it was too much to risk buying this old tug on the strength of some work in Barrow docks that we may not get. The owner must have sensed our reluctance to buy and knocked a large sum off the original price. We reached the sea, then when our bow started to lift in the North Sea swell, swung her around to head back up river to the Tyne bridge mooring. We had another more comprehensive inspection and everything seemed sound, even the bilges had been painted. The tug was immaculate, not a speck of rust anywhere, no expense had been spared on her construction.

This was a nice dream but not for us we were fishermen. We moored her back up saying to the owner we were not buying. He grabbed my hand knocking another huge lump off the asking price. "Bloody hell at this rate he will be paying us to take it off his hands!" I whispered to my partners, whilst the owner had a pee over the side. The man said "This is my final price and I will shake your hand on it!" The final price was a lot less than we received for the Easter Morn, it gave us one thousand pounds left over for our wages and expenses until we could get the tug back home to Barrow. We all shook on it, giving the Geordie a large deposit until we could get back to Newcastle with our gear. Strange we had the distinct impression he had robbed us and not the other way round!

Driving home it sank in that we three young lads were now the proud owners of a vintage old tug that had a bloody great funnel! Actually no work for her, we had let our enthusiasm run away with us!

Another adventure was about to begin and why did I have a sense of fore boding. We made a long list of gear and supplies back in Barrow for the long voyage up the east coast then through the Caledonian Canal and down the west coast home. It was winter severe bad weather was forecast so it might take some time to make the voyage back to Barrow. Strangely we never received any ship's papers or information about our boat nor after paying the man, ever see him again!

Always having to work to a very tight budget it was difficult to buy everything we would have wished, our beautiful brass compass had been stolen from the tug so a cheap plastic yacht one had to suffice. To make things worse our lovely wooden ships wheel was also pinched, we had it replaced with a smaller one. Our navigation aids were one compass, a couple of large scale charts, parallel rules and a Walker's trailing log. This trailed a brass propeller in the water behind our boat on a long line, to tell us the distance run, loaned to us by a friend. Fourteen very old lifejackets had been left behind on the boat which would probably sink if thrown in, a couple of old dodgy cork lifebuoys. So with my land rover loaded down with our gear and plenty of spare drums of red diesel for running around Newcastle we set off from Barrow, also with a friend to drive my motor back and a mate who wanted to be cook on the voyage home.

The weather was good for January so we expected to set off for home as soon as possible to take advantage of the calm before the gales started again. One of our partners was married and had children so we had to start earning as soon as possible. Pulling alongside the quay in Newcastle we looked down to see two men in suits pacing up and down the deck of our tug. Each man had a clipboard and each was writing furiously.

Climbing aboard we asked them "What the fuck are you doing on our boat without our permission?"

The taller of the two suits smirked and pointing to the wheelhouse door said "We do not need your permission we are from the Board of Trade that is a writ forbidding this boat to go to sea without my say so!"

It all became clear then why the Geordie man could not wait to off load the Argus onto us!

"You all seem a bit young to be owners of a boat this size" he said. I answered "This partner is the skipper he has a first mate ticket deep sea, the other is an engineer and I have been a skipper owner of a trawler for several years so what is your problem?" I said.

"My problem is the tugs lack of safety equipment, my colleague and myself have found sixty safety recommendations that must be addressed before you leave Newcastle!" The smug bastard could not stop smirking all this time, two right jobs worth.

"If you all decide to try and leave without our say so, the police launch will escort you back to face a severe penalty, good day to you all!"

Our skipper was the first to speak after looking at the rather extensive list of requirements "Fuck me we have been well and truly shafted lads!"

We sat in the charthouse and studied the lists in greater detail, the costliest item was a four man inflatable life raft, expensive in the past to buy or hire. A full set of charts which would cost a small fortune, flares and a line throwing gun, several fire extinguishers, spare this and spare that. All this equipment we were hoping to purchase in the future. Adding up a rough cost of the list was more than the tug cost us! Our future earnings were so unpredictable that we could not borrow money if we wanted to.

Sitting in our cosy cabin that night drinking a bottle or two of the famous Geordie jungle juice Newcastle brown ale, coal stove glowing red. We tried to form some sort of a plan. Brian said "Is this the end of our new venture so soon?" We then had our first break the Fishing News had an article about a local trawler sinking in the North Sea, all the crew after taking to the life raft were rescued by the local life boat. "Maybe the skipper still has the life raft" I said. That same day saw us knocking on a door in the next town asking a bemused man if he wanted to sell the raft that had saved his life. "No I do not it is in the garden the kids are going to use it for a paddling pool!"

After a few cups of tea and cake his lovely wife after hearing our story persuaded her husband to sell it to us cheaply. Feeling lucky for once we drove back with it to the tug. Getting it repacked at the factory was a sight cheaper than a new one. Back we drove to Barrow to see our friends in the coast guard service who lent us a line throwing gun and a shed load of flares, another mate found us our fire extinguishers, we did not ask where from. After ticking off the extensive list thanks to our friends and contacts in the coast guard, we loaded up the land rover and headed back to Newcastle for the final time hopefully! It was a good job we were using cheap red diesel the miles we had to do.

We phoned up the suits telling them the list was complied with and to come down to remove the writ off the boat, the man sounded very disappointed at my news. The next day the suits arrived and inspected what we had done then started to compile another new list. "What the hell do you think you are doing now?" I asked. "These hatches want three layers of canvas over them, some new oak wedges to make them water tight and sea worthy, plus there are other issues we need to discuss!"

The suits did not want the responsibility of letting us go, that or they were just a pair of bastards! We ordered them off the boat telling them we were sailing straight away, it was their fault we missed all the good weather, now thanks to them we were going to get the worst of the weather. We are not stopping for anyone, they were lucky we did not throw them into the river! They both stood on the quayside above us not saying a word glaring at us, looking miserable. Our engineer Brian started up the main engine, a cloud of black sooty smoke erupted from our funnel blowing over them, depositing a leaving present of large sooty particles on their once pristine white shirts. Now it was our turn to smirk!

We cast off the mooring ropes and headed full speed down river, determined to get started on our long journey home. Our ship's crew was increased by a friend on holiday coming as cook, so we had four men aboard. We came to the harbour mouth seeing a police launch hovering in mid channel. We did not slow down just called their bluff and ploughed on past it. A few scowls from them as we passed, heading full speed into a North Sea swell on our way, excited, apprehensive and sailing on a shoestring.

We had picked a bloody awful day to start our voyage, a big swell was rolling in, a freezing wind blew and the snow showers were getting heavier. The sky was grey the sea was grey I was thinking dark thoughts about the reliability of our engine. This adventure of ours could easily end in disaster but on the bright side having little money between us made us appreciate what we had! The stove was lit in the cabin, our cook was making his first meal getting used to working on a boat rolling in a beam sea. Skipper had first watch the engineer was in the warm engine room with his oil can. I was stowing away the mooring ropes and fenders getting ready for the bad weather expected soon. We had fitted a radio telephone in Newcastle to let the relevant coast guard stations know our progress hoping that would pacify the Board of Trade a little.

We headed northwards rolling heavily in rough waves the visibility was poor in the snow showers, everything looked bleak and dismal. I knew my mates were a bit apprehensive about whether this big engine in the tug was reliable or not, any break downs would be the end of our dreams all our hard work would be for nothing! It was the usual story we were on a wing and a prayer but were determined to enjoy every minute of our adventure. What always sustained me in my life was my belief in having a guardian angel always watching over me. Later that evening after standing my watch, I retired to my bunk for a couple of hours deciding to have a go for the very first time on my guitar, which was a birthday present from my sister. Getting carried away and being tone deaf

I plucked away alone in the cabin thinking I would not like to inflict this row on anyone at home. Occasionally I looked up to see inquisitive puzzled faces peering into the cabin from the top of the companion way ladder, but thought nothing of it at the time. These faces peering down looking anxious made me feel worried that something was going wrong on the boat. I thought that ten more minutes of plucking the strings then will go on deck to see what the problem was. Another ten minutes the ginger haired head of the engineer appeared, his face was bright red and after staring at me in my bunk his face grew redder, his eyes were bulging. He climbed quickly down into the cabin and grabbed the guitar out of my hands then ran straight back up the ladder without saying a word. Bloody strange behaviour I thought following him quickly onto the deck, I was just in time to see him on the stern of the tug throwing my guitar far into the waves! He saw me staring in amazement and said "You fucking prick I have spent ages trying to find the source of that terrible screeching noise in the engine room, I thought the main bearings were knackered or such like, even taking up the engine room floorings, I was crapping myself thinking the engine was fucked!" What could I say watching my birthday present floating away into the night it had been a very stressful few days!

We plodded on up the coast rock and rolling in the easterly gale, all decided to dock in Peterhead for a night. All moored up safely we sat around the mess room table looking forward to our volunteer cook's first main meal, mash, sausage and beans followed by tinned rice pudding.

Cook with a proud grin on his face dropped a large dollop of jam into the rice saying "This cooking lark is a piece of piss nothing to it!"

Very nice meal chef we all agreed, but this new fangled Cadbury's just add water potato mash tastes like shit compared to proper potatoes!

"Oh dear" was his reply. We were to find out soon what the 'Oh dear' meant. We were weather bound in Peterhead for three days and could not help noticing when we sailed into the North Sea on our way to Inverness that yet another meal consisted of mainly Cadbury's smash, we mentioned it to cook. "You ungrateful bastards you have had a variety, mash with sausage, bacon, beans, eggs, and even on toast what the hell more do you expect? I am a trained carpenter not a fucking cook!"

At this I opened the store cupboard and there were so many packs of Smash they were falling out onto the cabin floor. We gathered them up filling a fish basket and threw them all overboard into the sea. An indignant cook bleated about them being on offer half price he was only doing us a favour saving us money!

"Fucking real potatoes from now on or else! You could use that shite to plug a leak in the hull bottom" the skipper said.

Instead of going right around the top of Scotland we were going to use the Caledonian Canal which avoids the dangerous route across the Pentland Firth and its Skerries. The canal is one of the most scenic ones in the world cutting across Scotland from the North Sea to the West coast. Engineered by Thomas Telford and started in 1803 then finished in 1822, it takes a 150feet long ship with up to 35feet beam. Locks are twenty nine and the total length is 60 miles, only one third is manmade, the rest formed by Loch Dochfour, Oich and Lochy. The canal meant that shipping, mainly sail in those days could make the voyage quicker and more safely. The main engine was still running well and we had a rather brutal snow ball fight with the local kids which we lost. When locking through Neptunes Staircase near Fort William the weather was bitter cold with frequent snow showers, we never passed another boat. We fuelled up bought some stores in Oban then sailed through the Crinan Canal. Bad weather struck again and we were wind bound for a few more days in Campletown, time was against us so we decided to sail into atrocious sea conditions to finish the last leg south in the Irish Sea to our home port Barrow. We finally arrived home after experiencing some of the worst sea conditions we had ever seen on our long journey home.

Tied to the quay in Barrow we inspected the hull bottom and propeller at low tide, we were pleasantly surprised, the hull was in pristine condition likewise the propeller. We gave the hull three coats of black pitch and anti fouled the bottom. The insurance assessor inspected our tug and passed her with flying colours. The huge brass letters of Argus were chiselled off the stern her new name became 'Melanie Jane' after our skipper Stewart's new daughter. I wished he had just named her Jane, it was me that had to paint the long name on the stern, bows and all the lifebuoys, only joking Ann would have been even easier!

After giving the tug a complete refit we waited anxiously for our shipping agent friend to try and find us some work. We needed to put some food on our tables quickly. Sitting around the mess room table making one teabag do three cups with no biscuits to dunk, things as usual were looking a bit bleak to say the least. Then our saviour the shipping agent arrived onboard with great news, he had secured us our first charter in the docks, we could have kissed him. Our first job was assisting larger Liverpool tugs to tow a new nuclear submarine from one dock to another in a week's time. Remarkable that even in those days there were not any checks on our tug or us to make sure we could actually be trusted with one of Her Majesty's brand new nuclear submarines! We went to our trusty Wards ship breakers and luckily there was a navy frigate being scrapped, an advance off our agent bought us a lovely heavy nylon tow rope and steel hawser.

Bugger it! Thinking I would treat myself to a bright orange boiler suit to make myself look a little more respectable working on the tug's stern handling the tow rope. I wanted to look professional with hundreds of dock workers looking at our debut in the shipyard. My problem is being rather short arsed, only five feet five inches tall, when I tried the boiler suit on at home the legs were far too long, twelve inches needed to be cut off the bottom of each leg, the arms were ok though. My sister laughed saying she would do the cutting and sewing for me. Mother knew about our forth coming lucrative charter sensing a treat coming her way insisted that the job was hers. Reluctantly I handed her the boiler suit to alter overnight for the next day's charter. Picking them up the next morning on my way down to the tug I felt like the bees knee's as we say around here. Getting them out of the bag all the men on the quay wolf whistled, self consciously I put them on. Everyone pissed themselves laughing, I soon realised why! Mother had taken twelve inches off one leg only and taken twelve inches off one arm, she had totally fucked them up, I should have known better than to trust my mother with a sewing needle and scissors! Thank heavens nobody had a camera handy!

None of us had any experience of towing big heavy ships never mind being let loose on one of Her Majesties brand new nuclear submarines! We had visions of doing untold damage and being arrested for impersonating a tug company. Some hairy moments when the chief dock pilot asked our skipper to use maximum engine revolutions to help brake the sub to stop her crashing into the quay wall, black clouds erupted from the funnel converting white seagulls into black ones as they flew through our exhaust, but just in time we stopped her forward momentum. Our tug must have done a good job because the chief pilot called us up on the radio and said "Well done Melanie Jane thank you for doing an excellent job!"

My God we had got away with it. Several dock workers said it had been years since they had seen a coal fired steam tug working it was nice to see the smoke pouring from the funnel! We had a tot of rum as we steamed out of the dock entrance towards our mooring to celebrate our first dock charter. The chief dock pilot's praise boded well for future dock work. We did a few relaying mooring jobs and received another charter to assist moving a new build navy destroyer around the dock which went well. Only snag was we went alongside her putting a long dent in her side nobody seemed to notice so we did not say anything about it. Shortly after we received the unwelcome news that the ship yard had bought two new tugs of their own so no more dock work for us!

What to do now? A tug with no work equals a crew with no wages.

We sat around the table in our cabin having a meeting about converting our tug into a stern trawler. Of course the ideal way was to take the tug into a shipyard having the work done professionally. The bill would have been enormous this was not affordable in our wildest dreams. We three shipmates would have to do it all, beg, borrow and steal to make it into a paying success, failure and bankruptcy was not an option! First job was to have the Melanie Jane measured and allocated the number BW190, she was now registered for fishing. The numbers were painted on, now the hard part started, a trawl winch needed to be purchased. A stroke of luck for us a trawler was being scrapped at Fleetwood, we bought the trawl winch and with some modification it was fitted on the stern of our tug.

We luckily lived in the ideal place having all the pick of top class trades men who could weld, burn and make just about anything in Vickers shipyard. Some men helped us for cash and some for the promise of a feed of fish when we started fishing in the future. New mast, gallows and gantry were all made from metal bought or pinched from a scrap yard. The huge hole left in the fore deck after removing the chart house was plated and welded up by one of the finest tradesmen ever in Vickers. His name is Joe eventually receiving the MBE in recognition for a lifetime of shipbuilding excellence, a cracking man we were proud to call him a friend.

The two lifting derricks needed were a problem this dilemma was solved by a good friend in the Highways Department. He placed two brand new street lighting poles next to a hole in the perimeter fence, so on a stormy, rain swept night we managed to lift them onto my trusty land rover. Keeping our fingers crossed that the local Bobbies were sheltering indoors somewhere warm and dry supping tea. We transported them down to the boat the only problem was the huge dent in the land rovers cab! The two twenty feet long lighting poles were perfect for the job, lugs for the shackles were welded on, deck lights obtained from a scrapped trawler were fixed on top. The tug was slowly becoming to look like a stern trawler. A shame the toilet compartment had to be removed to make room for a bigger fish room, it was back to using a bucket in the engine room, but at least it was warm if a little noisy. Yet again the many aluminium fish pound boards salvaged from the Stephil came in useful for our new fish room. We now had room for storing ice so that we could do five day trips if necessary. The conversion work took several weeks with no wages coming in as usual it was a struggle. I think we were all getting quay crazy listening on the radio about all the big landings the Fleetwood boats were bringing in. At last the day arrived when we could head out to sea to give the boat a trawling trial, we had new wooden otter boards made locally by a mate in his backyard, a brand new Boris trawl net from Fleetwood and a second hand prawn trawl.

A lovely feeling at high water to have the Jubilee Bridge lifted and proudly steam through, not that the double decked buses, taxis and dozens of cars would probably agree or the many pedestrians being held up. Steaming past Vicker's launching slips the lads working on a nuclear submarine and a navy destroyer all gave us a wave, most of them had given us help in some way to get us back to sea without them we would have been scuppered. The first catch would have to be shared out to a lot of people.

We needed to test the winch drives and could only do this with an actual trial run, so were apprehensive when we shot the trawl one hour southwest of Lightning Knoll on a choppy day. We thought it prudent to only tow for thirty minutes instead of the usual three hour tows. Here goes we thought as the weight was put on the winch for the first time to pull it back off the seabed. A loud bang and we knew the drive on the shaft had snapped off, we were fucked! Our system was just not up to the job, we needed to go back to the drawing board.

The trawl was on the bottom of the sea bed including two otter doors, bridles and three hundred feet a side of steel trawl warps, weighing a considerable amount, all unfortunately lying in over one hundred feet of water. The first thought was to call up another trawler to ask them to come alongside to use their winch but typically the horizon was empty, the forecast was for severe gales approaching so we had a very small weather window to lift it all somehow, or mark it and leave it. Skipper came up with a good idea using rope block and tackles, putting strops around the warps we could get a lift of sixty feet a time along our deck, hard work with the boat rolling badly in the ever increasing wind.

All night we worked without a break pulling everything back aboard ever so slowly, until at last we lifted the last part onboard being the cod end, even after a thirty minute tow there were two baskets of plaice, three of cod a full basket of whelks. This boded well for the future, these fish we had were spoken for they would soon be in the hands of our helpers. The big heap of tangled gear on our deck would take hours to untangle, a new stronger sleeve would have to be welded onto the winch drive, another job for Joe! We had recovered our gear just in time, the storm front rolled in as predicted our boat receiving a right pasting heading back to Barrow.

While we had the trawl gear on the quayside sorting it out Joe was making sure that the problem would not happen again, soon we were ready to try again. We sailed again this time managing to have two successful three hour tows then steamed across the bay toward Fleetwood. Everything on our boat seemed to be working fine thank goodness and we landed our small maiden catch. When the Fleetwood lads saw our tug conversion they were merciless with their piss taking, the tall funnel made them laugh, they straight away nick named our boat 'African Queen.' We could not blame them too much, nobody had ever heard of a tug being converted into a stern trawler before, she was unique, we would just have to show them we could catch fish just as well as any conventional trawler.

At least we did not have the bank owning part of our boat, we three young lads owned it outright for better or for worse. Our boat may have looked ugly but we three partners were very proud of her, having belief that she would provide for our three families. We had a position finding Decca Navigator fitted to plot where we fished installed it was expensive to rent but necessary. We fuelled up all our diesel tanks, bought new fish baskets, oilskins, gutting knives, had stores delivered to our ship for a five day trip into the Irish Sea. We had everything on our account adding up to a load of money, this was last chance saloon for us, one unsuccessful trip and we were bankrupt. Last job before leaving Fleetwood was to fill up with flake ice for keeping the fish fresh. We just hoped and prayed that our boat's engine was up to running continually for five days nonstop, without breaking down! Our business success was always on a knife edge, nobody could say we did not try!

Filled with optimism we sailed out of the lock gates in the company of deep sea, middle water and many inshore boats to find some fish! The sight of so many colourful fishing vessels all leaving Fleetwood on the ebb tide never failed to move me, I was proud to call myself a fisherman.

There was a plentiful supply of pain killers in my locker and I certainly needed them over the next five days. Hauling in the trawl every three hours, day and night was the hardest job I could ever imagine. Every time the cod end was emptied the trawl was immediately put back over the stern for another tow. The boat was only earning money with the net over the side. Sorting and gutting fish, washing them thoroughly to get out the last bits of liver and blood, then go below into the fish room to pack them in ice in the pounds. This routine went on hour after hour. We were certainly on the fish, by the time we had finished gutting and clearing them down below it was nearly time to haul again.

To feed us I had a huge pan sitting on a low light on the stove, filled with vegetables, tinned meat, potatoes and gravy bubbling away, anyone could just help themselves when required. Brews were on the go all the time. Sitting on the fish room hatch gutting thousands of plaice in pouring rain, constant soakings from spray in rough seas day and night, it certainly was not for the feint hearted. We all loved every minute not wanting to trade places with anyone. Sometimes another trawler would steam alongside to ask how we were getting on, borrow a spare packet of tea, or a five gallon drum of oil. We were amazed that we trawled day and night for five days without anything dropping off the engine or breaking down.

Our fish room was full at long last, we were all sick of my stew which I had kept topped up for days. The skipper threw the contents left over the side on the way in, giving the seagulls a treat. We had some bad weather on this trip but stuck it out a full fish room being our just reward. Our Melanie Jane shut the piss takers up when we landed seventy baskets of plaice, a heap of cod, some prime turbot, plus eight boxes of dover soles into Fleetwood market. Being the shortest I drew the short straw and was nominated to work in the fish hold which did not have much head room. My back problem became worse with my promotion to the bowels of our fish room! This entailed filling baskets with fish from the pounds and hooking them ready to hoist up. The engineer operated the landing derrick, skipper emptying the baskets into boxes and stacking them up on the quayside ready to be collected. We finally achieved some decent wages after all this time and hard work.

Everybody was happy with our first trip all agreed it was worth it. For the first and last time we landed onto a market with all the fish prices sky high. Paying off all our outstanding bills was a great feeling. That night in Fleetwood was celebrated in the Chinese restaurant and yes the staff recognised me, even shaking hands, we toasted the Melanie Jane's success.

My money from our first few trips was spent putting a new bathroom in my parent's house and modernising it. They were pensioners now and deserved a little bit of comfort in their old age.

Steaming out from Barrow one afternoon we saw two Fleetwood trawlers on the horizon, the skippers conversation on the radio went like this "See the African Queen is on her way out of Barrow!"

"How do you know it is them?"

"The seagulls flying past me are covered in soot!"

Very witty we thought at least we gave them a laugh!

The only way to get our own back was by showing them we could catch fish. Typically after landing consistently good catches we started having costly breakdowns, then one day two of us nearly drowned.

We were sailing past Lightning Knoll buoy on a calm hazy summer day when our main engine just spluttered then stopped for no apparent reason. There was a lazy swell it was stifling hot, skipper and engineer went down into the engine room to find the cause of the break down. Onboard was the young lad working for us that swam out to fetch the inflatable when salvaging the Stephil wreck. We passed the lads in the engine room a jug of cool orange while waiting on deck, the sweat pouring off us. The boat was not drifting much it was low water so did not bother to drop the anchor. "Let's go over the side for a swim to cool off" my young friend said. Next minute we were swimming around the boat in our underpants, thinking what a hell hole that engine room must be like.

The boat was just wallowing slowly from side to side occasionally banging noises could be heard above the racket of Radio One belting out over the loud speaker. Our young friend liked his pop music! The tide was starting to flood in now so we were both heading back towards the boat. We were further away than was sensible but making good progress. We had not mentioned our intentions to the others about our going over the side for a swim, which was very silly of us.

You would not believe what happened next a huge swarm of Barrel jellyfish appeared between us and the boat. These jellyfish are the average size of footballs and weigh very heavy. We had to do the breaststroke just to fend them off from hitting our faces, of course our progress forwards had stopped, and we were going slowly further away from our boat. It was no good shouting with the radio blasting the music out and what if they could not repair the engine? We could have drifted miles away into the haze before anyone realised we were not on board. My friend started to have a panic attack when jelly after jelly bumped into us feeling like being stung by hundreds of nettles.

They swarm in their thousands in the summertime are large, transparent domed-shaped, the sting being underneath in the tentacles. They are very heavy weighing up to forty pounds and a beautiful pearl colour. Sometimes they wash into Morecambe bay then are left in their thousands to ebb out on the sands to shrivel and dry out in the sun, a sad end after their long voyage. We call them locally Barrel jellyfish their sting is very irritating.

"Bloody hell this looks bad for us, two silly sods drowned off the Knoll covered head to toe in fucking jellyfish stings!" I said.

The banging had finished a lone figure appeared on deck taking a leak over the side, we both started yelling and waving our arms in the air to attract his attention. Suddenly he was running to the engine room.

"If the engine is not repaired we are up shit creek without a paddle Norm!"

"That's answered your question" I said.

A roar, then a huge black mushroom cloud erupted from the funnel, from out of the cloud sailed our Melanie Jane looking a beautiful sight! After we had been rescued skipper said "You know that you both would have been brown bread if we had not just managed to fix the engine or if you had not been spotted in time, you are both prize dick heads!" Who could argue with that! We both had a wash down with fresh water which alleviates the pain of the jellyfish stings. The next few days the Calamine lotion was plastered on, the angry red blotches on our bodies disappeared we were soon back to normal.

When the engine and other bits were working all right we managed to make decent wages, what with one thing and another you could say there was never a dull moment in our lives. Looking back I remember one winter's night we were towing along off Saint Bees Head picking up some very large cod full of roe (eggs). Our skipper had earlier passed me up a plate of boiled cod roe, he and the engineer were both off watch in their bunks. About two o'clock in the morning I was still on watch feeling a little drowsy, in another hour I would wake the lads with a brew and pick up the trawl once again. I was expecting a good haul of cod the fish finder had shown up some good marks. Some of the trawlers fishing nearby had reported hauls of thirty baskets of large cod.

The deck was covered in a layer of white hoar frost so it was not pitch black, I could see the fishing lights of several Fleetwood and Whitehaven trawlers all having a bonanza on the cod. Looking up from the compass I could see a dark figure stood on the starboard bow, at first I thought one of the crew was having a pee over the side. Then I realised that nobody could have come past me without my noticing, it was the only exit from the cabin and it was in front of me. Quickly I went into the cabin seeing my two crew mates still in their bunks, both snoring like pigs. Then I went back to look out of the wheelhouse window. The tall black shape was still there on the starboard side bow looking forwards with his back to me. Opening the wheelhouse door I climbed down the steps to deck level, the moon had come out from behind the clouds everywhere looked brighter. Now the hairs stood up on the back of my neck, I had half believed up to then that it was just a shadow I was seeing now I knew it was not. The front of the boat was light and no shadows were being cast, there was only this tall figure dressed all in black. Dashing down the steps into the cabin, I woke the crew telling them it was time to haul up the trawl. My hope was that they would see the apparition still on the bow when they went on deck. I stayed down below with them until we all stepped outside dressed in our waterproofs, the skipper commented on how pale I looked and did I feel all right? Looking at the front of the boat it was now pitch black, the moon was back behind the clouds.

For fear of ridicule I never mentioned the man in black to anyone until now. A curious thing happened years later when I was in Whitby on the east coast, talking to an angler fishing on the pier. He told me he used to go on deepwater fishing trips on an old black tug from Newcastle many years ago which was supposed to be haunted by a man who lost his life on board! The boat was not particularly unlucky for us but when we eventually sold her the new owner drowned, and I believe she later set on fire and sank in deep water off the Western Isles of Scotland!

After a few more trawling trips we were tied up at our usual quay wall in Barrow with engine problems, this time it was really serious.

The Ruston main engine had five cylinders with five huge pistons, one of the conrods was broken. This part was very expensive and difficult to get hold of, also we were broke with the bank account empty. This was really annoying because the Fleetwood, Whitehaven and Irish trawlers were making record catches of Dublin bay prawns, we could hear them talking from the radio left on in the wheelhouse. Even if the boat was tied up in Barrow not working, the bills and overheads were mounting up fast. Fleetwood dock dues, insurance, fish agents fees, Decca rental still to be paid and three families that relied on us, a difficult situation! We were all sat around the mess room table actually talking about the possibility of going bankrupt, which pissed me off because we always busted a gut trying to make a success of our venture, we were all grafters every time we were doing well the engine let us down. A case of one step forward and two steps back all the time. Sometimes in life you are thrown a lifeline fate steps in and gives you one last chance! The voice of our shipping agent shouted that he was coming aboard with some news for us.

We could tell he was excited I shoved a mug of tea into his hand.

"I have got the perfect charter for you, a very interesting job and a great bonus at the end of it!" he said.

"There is a coaster aground in the Duddon estuary carrying a cargo of scrap iron, her name is 'Action' and believe me she has seen some lately!"

"She needs a tow off the sand bank and towing or assisting back to Barrow docks on tomorrow afternoon tide, you are the only tug available in this area at short notice."

"By the way she loaded her cargo at Fleetwood, went into Barrow docks with engine trouble, left for her destination Cork in Ireland, ending up in the Duddon estuary with more engine problems even losing one of her anchors!"

My thought was bloody hell a ship worse off than ours!

"Well the charter rate is very generous so what do you say?"

On the point of saying no we are out of commission, Brian the engineer kicked me hard on the shin under the table and said to the agent "Tell the 'Action' captain to be ready tomorrow to receive our tow rope one hour

before high tide, I will have a quick look at his engines before we set off."
Me! I just looked at our engineer in amazement.

The agent shook hands with us all, said what a fine ship we had and left.

Our skipper said "How on earth are we going to do this charter when our boat is out of commission?"

"Our engineer said "If you think I am going under without a fight think again, without the engine this boat is only worth scrap value!"

"Working all night we will disconnect the conrod and lash the piston in the cylinder head with lashing wire and run the engine with just four cylinders. We will get this charter done the money earned will pay for a permanent engine repair and get us back to fishing earning wages!"

"What happens if the lashing wire comes adrift and the piston falls into the crank shaft when we are steaming at full speed?" I said.

"Then we are in deep shit Norm! Have you a better suggestion?" I had an awful vision of the huge piston coming adrift falling into the crankshaft, the engine blowing up, our boat sinking, three partners sitting in a life raft contemplating our career options.

The next day saw us steaming north along the Walney coastline towards the treacherous shallow Duddon estuary. This is where the channels are constantly changing from one week to another making pilotage a nightmare. Also a huge sand bar forms at the entrance to the estuary shifting in height and depth almost daily. This is not a sensible place for a tug or coaster to be caught out especially in bad weather. Now I realised why all the other tugs in the Irish Sea declined the charter, they were obviously not that desperate for work. My bet was they heard the mention of the Duddon estuary immediately putting the phone down! For the next few hours the forecast was favourable SW4 to SW5. If we did not hang about or have any unforeseen problems we would be in and out of the estuary quickly before the gale arrived. We crossed the bar with not much water under our keel and a little nail biting.

Heading further into shallower water, we were wondering how the coaster managed to get into the narrow twisting channel leading to Roan head nature reserve in the dark. They too must have had a guardian angel looking after them. The Action laid in a narrow channel, on one side a sand bar, on the other miles of sand banks and small gulley's. She was lying to her one remaining anchor losing the other one near Millom pier the day before. We tied alongside quickly introduced ourselves to the owner of the Action and his pretty young wife, also the captain and deckhand/ engineer. We coupled up our tow and lifted their anchor manually using the windlass, our engineer got both their engines going but they both ran erratically. Time was pressing on, so with a last check that everything on the coaster was stowed ready for the possibility of worsening weather, we slowly started to tow the Action towards the bar. The spring high tide had passed and the ebb was beginning to run out fast, the sky to the west was inky black already dusk was approaching. The wind was increasing it would be wind against tide, our engine was running well and with the tide with us we were making good progress. We had an extra experienced deckhand with us thank goodness we would need him.

This ever changing estuary has been a death trap for many a sailing ship in the past years, many a fine vessel has been wrecked attempting to cross over the bar. These ships delivered pit props and such like for the Hodbarrow iron ore mines at Millom and to misjudge the depth of water was catastrophic. The anchor off the schooner Coniston was salvaged in 1975, she was heading into the estuary with a cargo of pit props unfortunately her skipper misjudged the water over the bar, she touched on and rolled completely over in seconds ripping out her two masts, leaving the estuary strewn with larch pit props. Tragically there were no survivors that escaped from the Coniston, the rest of her cargo was salvaged by cutting holes in the bottom of her hull. Many lost anchors from these wrecks have been trawled up over the years by local fishing boats and many wrecks are waiting to be uncovered by the constantly changing sands.

Halfway to the bar the tow rope broke due to chafing on the Actions bow and her helmsman not keeping a steady course. We pulled in the snapped warp passing over another quickly. The wind had increased dramatically the visibility was getting worse in the rain squalls, we had nearly reached the bar when the tow parted at the coasters bow again. The Actions captain radioed that he would try to reconnect one more time as her decks were constantly being swept by waves.

Skipper called up the coast guard asking Barrow lifeboat to stand by if we needed them to launch, they said that they were happy enough to wait and see how we got on with the next attempt to reconnect. We connected up again with great difficulty in the poor visibility and pulled her bow around on course again. Slowly we made our way towards the bar then hopefully into deeper water. The seas were foaming on the bar and we could see where to cross it in safety. Unfortunately the coaster touched on the sandy bottom in a trough the tow parting once more, whipping back knocking me and our deckhand into a heap in the scuppers. We were both hurt the rope had whipped across our backs as we ducked down. No time to dwell on it though, but had to get up to pull the loose warp back aboard quickly. If it fouled our propeller we would be in imminent danger of being swept broad side on to the waves and swamped, or rolled over, unable to rescue the coasters crew.

The coaster was swept broadside to the seas, waves were washing clean over her wheel house we could see the diffused glow from her navigation lights under the water. The captain was in a panic radioing to be taken off right away. We ran the Melanie Jane straight alongside for them to jump aboard stoving in and splitting our gunnels. Our skipper showed superb seamanship managing to hold her there long enough for their engineer to clamber onto our deck. There was no use Barrow lifeboat launching as they were miles away and the rescue had to happen now, but they were on standby just in case. Just then the gearbox control from the wheel house to the engine room snapped this meant our engineer had to stay in the engine room and a crew member had to shout down the skipper's instructions from the deck. This left just one of us on deck to help pull the Actions crew onto the safety of our boat. Trying to come alongside again, the coaster rolled our way and we sat on top of her deck flattening her railings, the next wave washed us off again. We had time to pull the owner aboard his wife jumped slipping between both hulls. The boats crashed together it looked like her legs may have been crushed, luckily our trawl gallows stuck out far enough to make a gap for her legs, I pulled her aboard gasping like a fish but safe!

We sailed around one more time in the dark our skipper put our stern under their stern, we shouted for the last man to jump onto our trawl net to help cushion his fall. The crew were all suffering from shock and seasickness but safe. We put blankets around them giving them mugs of sweet tea then taking them down below where it was warm. Skipper radioed for an ambulance to meet us at Barrow docks.

The coast guard put a message out to all shipping that an abandoned coaster was drifting in the Irish Sea. Barrow lifeboat crew kindly stood by until we safely neared the shelter of Walney channel. The last view of the Action that night was huge rolling waves crashing right over her, the lifeboat being torn off her deck and washed away. The wind was screaming now our boat received a real pasting that night ploughing her way to the safety of Barrow docks, a real tribute to the shipyard who had built her all those years ago. The faithful old Ruston Hornsby diesel engine running sweetly on only four cylinders never missing a beat and not letting us down. Somebody was looking after us that awful night!

Melanie Jane was safely tucked up in her berth at Ferry beach it was time to search for our abandoned coaster. Heaven only knows whether she had sunk, was drifting about somewhere in the Irish Sea or washed ashore. My friend went up in his aeroplane to see if he could spot her, thus saving me a lot of time and effort by discovering Action was aground in the estuary again. We went to Roan Head luckily the sand was firm enough to motor out in the trusty land rover right up to her. The poor ship looked battered, loose ropes and halliards were blowing horizontal in the howling wind. Our first priority was to hire a local tractor to tow out the anchor and cable towards deep water to stop her washing further inshore. Then we replaced the canvas hatch covers and put new wooden wedges back in place that had washed out. She had obviously spent more time under water last night than above, loose ropes were wrapped around the tips of the mast. A nice surprise when we sounded the bilges, no water was aboard her, a good start. A Customs officer turned up with our agent both climbed up the rope ladder to come aboard. The agent had a message from the owner of the Action thanking us for saving their lives, saying they would not have believed how ferocious the seas had been if not seeing with their own eyes! They felt very lucky to be alive!

The insurance company asked us to try and salvage the Action and if successful to tow her into Barrow docks, also they would pay us a daily rate which we accepted. Typically the shipping forecast for the foreseeable future was Westerly winds storm force nine to ten. A few more spring tides and she would be neaped so we prepared to have another attempt at towing her off. First problem was the huge sand bank building up on one side of the boat, looking under the hull we could see some dented plates on the bottom, but she was not leaking.

Two excavators we hired removed the entire sandbank around her, and made a deep channel leading out to her anchor. There was a short weather window before the next low pressure system, so we steamed into the estuary once more with a little trepidation I must admit. We had a lucky escape last time the consolation now was only our crew would be on both boats the owner and his crew had washed their hands of it. They had their personal possessions taken off and delivered to them by the shipping agent. Our engineer had worked hard on both of the coasters engines and they were running alright now, we came alongside her and connected up a tow line, then lifted up the Actions anchor. We started to take the strain with both engines on the coaster on full power and us using all ours. Action began to move slowly ahead, we started to head for the deeper channel leading out to sea. A short time later Action touched on again refusing to go further, just not having enough water under her keel. We laid out the Action's anchor once again, just managing to get over the bar ourselves, touching on occasionally, our keel kicking up sand when the huge swell rolling in dropped us in a trough. We steamed for home to try again when the tides were suitable.

The next storm arrived and when we boarded her at low water we could see she had taken a right hammering, all the stanchions were flattened the wooden hatch covers and all canvas covers had washed away. The holds were full of seawater and the hull was leaking in different places.

We had a couple of visits from hovercraft that were built in the factory in Millom to see if they could be of any assistance to us, which was very kind of them. The pilot of one of the hovercraft told me it took just one hundred seconds to cross from Millom beach to Askam pier and only ten minutes to Walney bridge a remarkable speed. He gave me a demonstration to prove it. Sadly this company went out of business in Millom, leaving many unemployed.

The insurance assessor called a meeting and we were offered our fee or we could keep the coaster. After carefully weighing things up we accepted the charter fee it would be a big risk to try any longer to salvage her, we were happy and the owner was happy. The owner of the Action bought a beautiful modern cargo boat and never looked back. The Action was bought by a local plant hire man who had all the equipment to unload the cargo of scrap quickly where she laid, then when the holds were empty tow it up the beach, selling the engines, and burning the boat up for scrap on the high water mark.

We managed to find a spare engine for Melanie Jane in Bristol docks that had been used in an ex fire fighting boat. We hired a lorry and spent all night aboard the fire float stripping the main engine of bits to bring back to Barrow. Our brilliant engineer Brian fixed the engine, at last we were back to normal service, this was our last towing charter for money, all the other towing afterwards consisted of bringing friend's trawlers back to port with trawl nets or ropes around their propellers, or engine break downs.

The biggest thrill from fishing I ever have over the years is when each time the trawl is hauled, you look in anticipation to see what empties out of the cod end, never being sure what you will find. Giant old schooner anchors, old shells and bombs dumped at sea after the two world wars crop up quite frequently, bits off old wrecks and the odd giant fish like the monkfish we once caught. We lifted it with a block and tackle into a forty gallon drum head first and its tail came over the top and onto the deck! The strangest haul was off the port of Whitehaven, I was sorting through the catch, coming across a shiny polished, brown leather man's shoe with a sock still inside. I picked off the whelks from inside the sock to throw in the basket noticing it looked like a bone sticking up with flesh around it. Throwing it across to my deck mate I asked him to confirm if it was a human foot and ankle? He prodded it, stared at it, then threw it overboard saying "Your right Norm it is a human foot I wonder who it belonged to?"

"We will never know now will we!" I answered.

At this time several large twin beam trawlers from Holland were fishing just outside the British twelve mile limit catching large quantities of dover soles, a very high value fish. A few of the Barrow boats decided to give this mode of fishing a try which involved towing a very heavy beam trawl on either side of the boat, the mouth of the net had heavy chains that dug into the mud of the seabed digging out huge dover soles. Two of us went on a few trips when the regular crew were on holiday or sick leave to see what this kind of fishing was like, also because the wages were high. It was certainly an eye opener for me, we had to haul every two hours at the most, sometimes after just one hour the nets were full of mud and starfish, two nets fishing at the same time equals two cod ends full and took some shovelling back over the side! Tie up the cod ends and over the side again, then delve into the heap of corruption, digging soles out of the shite, maybe a half hour exhausted sleep before the skipper woke us up with his hunting horn, then the whole process started over again.

This was no fun, fishing until we were all dead on our feet, clearing and sorting the catch left no time for a proper rest, this was twenty four hours a day. Sometimes we had to tow the nets at full speed through the water they were so full of glutinous mud in order to swill some out, making the cod end lighter.

One trip I will never forget was after fishing on this boat for twenty four hours, needing to haul every hour we were absolutely knackered. Our skipper had a call for help from a fellow skipper of a large trawler from Fleetwood who had his trawl net stuck on the bottom and an engine breakdown. He had no means of retrieving it and needed a tow home to Fleetwood. This was about two o'clock in the morning pouring with rain and blowing a bastard, sea very rough. Our skipper insisted we haul our gear just as we were hammering the soles. He wanted to use our winch to haul his mate's gear onto our deck, then transfer it back onto his mate's boat, and then tow him to Fleetwood!

We told our skipper to tell the Fleetwood lad to put a buoy on it to mark it, then to come back for it when he had his engine repaired. Our skipper told us to 'fuck off' and do as we were told. Well you can imagine what a job we had in those sea conditions hauling up the other trawler's full set of gear off the seabed, after he had passed the end of his trawl wires over. We were absolutely worn out when we had the last of his gear aboard us in a great big heap. We steamed across to him and connected a tow rope up, while the skipper steered towards Fleetwood we still had our last haul to gut and get below, it was still pouring down, both boats were rolling their side decks under in the heavy sea.

Well we thought when we get into Fleetwood, we can transfer this guy's trawl net, otter doors and fathom after fathom of trawl warps, get our heads down for eight hours then come back out on the next tide, after all we had earned a rest. We got the other boat safely tied up in the dock including all his gear back aboard, then said to our skipper "This has been a long night" his answer was "It's not finished yet Norm get the gear ready for shooting away, we are going straight back out!"

"The bastard"

We were glad to get back to fishing our Melanie Jane. A young school boy called Jimmy started to call down to our boat asking if we needed any help, it was obvious he was mad on boats. Jimmy started off with us letting him brew up and clean our galley, later he began to show an interest in learning how to splice rope. Most school boys who came down Ferry beach soon got fed up and you would not see them again, not this lad. He progressed to me showing him how to mend trawl nets, tie knots, read a compass taking a keen interest in all things nautical. At the start of the school holidays Jimmy asked me if he could come out on trawling trips with us and stay with us all summer. We said no it was too much responsibility for us to take on, I could see Jimmy was really disappointed. Next he begged me to take him home to see his mother to talk about it. Throwing his bicycle into the land rover I took Jimmy home, meeting his lovely mother. After interrogating me for an hour she said it was alright for little Jimmy to spend his summer holidays with us on the boat, the look on his face was priceless. Every time we landed in Fleetwood I made sure Jimmy phoned home, I must say he was a good shipmate and popular with everyone. When Jimmy grew up he entered the Royal Navy and served with distinction in the Falklands war, all these years later he is captain of a wind farm support vessel, followed on by his son, who is also a captain in the Merchant Navy. Needless to say I am very proud of them both.

There was a big end of season games competition coming up at our sailing club we had a large bet on me winning the pool final. We thought it was a good idea to have a few practice games one dark and stormy night, knowing we would not be disturbed in the club house. One of our mates was on the committee so had his own key, he let us in and after having a brew we started putting our twenty pence's into the pool table. Soon we ran out of money and our committee man said if two of them lifted up the slate top, I could put my hand under and grab a handful of coins so we could carry on playing. "It's not as if we are stealing because we are going to put all the money back in" he said. Adding that this was a common practice, that nobody would be visiting the club on a shitty night like this. They both lifted up the heavy slate top and I slid my arm down, my hand felt the heap of coins in the cash box and grabbing a handful shouted "Success!"

Just at that moment our committee man spotted car headlights approaching the club house. He panicked and let go of the pool table top, running out of the door saying he could not afford to be seen with someone stealing from club property! My best mate could not hold the weight he dropped it, running out the door shouting that it was no good three of us being done for stealing! Firstly my trapped arm was very painful and could be crushed. Secondly I had been a member for many years so felt embarrassed if the footsteps approaching belonged to the Commodore. The club house door opened and to my great relief saw that it was a friend of ours. Seeing the compromising position I was in he burst out laughing. I shouted to him "get outside and find the other two cowardly ex friends of mine before I lose my fucking arm!" After a few minutes my two sheepish spineless mates strolled in to the clubhouse apologising profusely, but would not lift the pool table top off my arm before making sure I still had the coins in my fist! What a wasted effort, I had to drop out of the competition due to swelling of the fingers and a badly bruised arm.

The crew's cabin on our Melanie Jane was huge compared to a traditional fishing boat, many a time it was crammed full of fishermen. After landing our catch in the early hours of the morning in Fleetwood docks, instead of going home straight away sometimes everyone would pile into our forward cabin for a yarn. Over mugs of coffee and bacon buns all round we would chat, sometimes one of the lads would have his guitar and a singsong would commence. These old trawler men had some great stories to tell especially when the rum bottle was produced. Happy days, the old characters have gone and their boats have been scrapped, only our memories now.

Casting off the mooring ropes before dawn it was looking like being a lovely day. The previous week had been gale after gale rolling into the

Irish Sea. The sun was rising in the east casting a beautiful red glow to the few low clouds drifting slowly along. This was a day when all the previous bad weather and no wages was forgotten, a day when you would not swap places with anyone on earth. We were hunting for the mackerel shoals and they could be anywhere. Cruising slowly up the coast northwards we spotted the gannets diving, we knew then that we had found a shoal. The echo sounder showed a dense mass of fish under the boat and very near the surface. We each dropped our hand lines of ten feathers over the side. Each line weighted with a pound of lead, the ravenous fish were fighting to hook themselves. Line after full line was quickly pulled aboard and the ten fish a time shaken off into the fish pounds. This procedure was repeated until the fish pound was full, our arms and fingers aching.

Time for a hose down to remove all the blood and gore from our faces and oilskins. Clean and fill the boxes with these beautiful fish then time for a well deserved mug of tea. Even if the weather changes for the worse we have earned some money to tide us over for another week. The gulls are still striding around our deck pinching the odd mackerel completely unafraid of us, seeming to know we do not begrudge them the odd fish. Young Jimmy is on the wheel proud as punch that we trust him to point our bow towards the tiny white speck of Walney lighthouse in the far distance and steam for home. Meanwhile we all sit with our backs against the tall warm funnel having a well earned rest enjoying a mug of tea.

Fishing from Barrow were a few larger boats at this time, consisting of sixty foot trawlers named the Vertrouwen, Wendy Ann, Arie Dirk, Melanie Jane, and the wooden Saint Pierre which we had towed in due to an engine breakdown. She received a battering at Belfast berth during a storm and sank. Later she was salvaged and towed to North Scale, unfortunately she never sailed again. A successful charity night was held in the Nautical Club on Walney to help the two young lads who owned her pay for the salvage cost. A later addition to the fleet was Lady Marjory another big steel trawler who was eventually sold to Brixham.

Due to the price of fuel oil rocketing and low fish prices, one by one the boats were sold, the fuel price affected us so badly we were doing sixty basket trips just to pay for overheads, so decided reluctantly to put her up for sale. The Fleetwood trawlers were being sold off gradually suffering from the same problems as us. A smashing young lad from Stornaway in the Western Isles bought our boat for scallop diving and salvaging wrecks. We heard later that the poor lad had been drowned, sometime later the boat had set on fire and sunk somewhere off the Western Isles. We were sad parting with our beloved boat she had served us well. We had all these adventures on her, shared by good ship mates, but it was now time to go our separate ways.

CHAPTER SEVENTEEN

My health was suffering at this time, a trawler man's life is hard enough when fit, having to take large doses of pain killers for years to keep going had caught up with me, and I desperately needed a break from fishing.

Fate again strikes when you least expect it, standing at the bar one night in the Bay Horse pondering what to do with my life, spotted an old school friend I had not seen for many years. My old friend had recently been discharged from the army the last few months had been running adventure trips to Morocco, using an ex London double deck bus carrying twelve people at a time. He started telling me tales of his adventures, like the trip he made with twelve Swedish girls, reckoning he had slept with ten of them during the two week trip.

"If these trips were so much fun what are you doing back in Barrow propping up the bar mate" I said.

"I put all my army savings into buying that bloody bus and had to leave it in Morocco with a seized up engine. Having no money to repair means it will be just a looted carcass now. The tourist party with me had a lift home on another tour bus and I eventually hitched home, really need to look for a job quick"

Thinking that I would buy a long wheelbase safari land rover and do the same trip, I asked him if he wanted to come with me for a free holiday. The deal was that I would pay all his expenses. It sounded like a good break for me and an adventure with a good mate who had been to Morocco before. Bill agreed and after a few pints I left with his contact address, promising to get in touch when I had purchased my new land rover. Eventually I found my dream safari land rover in Manchester that had every extra fitted that money could buy. Twelve seats, petrol engine, even equipped with a capstan winch on the front, which I knew would come in handy for the desert. That was all my share of the Melanie Jane gone, another chapter starting.

Loading up with supplies and spare fuel /water containers we set off for Dover and the ferry to France. First stop Paris and I was not disappointed, we parked our motor at a small cheap hotel by the Rue Saint Denis one of the oldest streets in the city used by prostitutes from the Middle Ages to this day we were reliably informed. Later we visited Notre Dame cathedral, had lunch near the Louvre and a trip to the top of the Eiffel Tower. The meal we had on the Avenue Des Champs Elyees was wonderful, sitting imagining when the German troops were goose stepping through the Paris streets, made history come alive. Soon it was time to move on to Lyon, Toulouse then into Biarritz. What a place that was, beautiful women and flashy sports cars, we could not afford to buy an ice cream in that place. After a sun bathe and a swim it was time to head off again.

Heading into Spain we drove to Madrid and visited the Royal Palace, the largest royal palace in Europe, sat in the Plaza de Oriente the beautiful square eating tapas, sampling the fine Manzanilla sherry. We looked around the cathedral and after a huge dinner both fell asleep in the back of the land rover. The next morning up early and keen to set off, we headed for Seville and onto Algeciras, to catch the ferry across the strait to Ceuta, eighteen miles from Gibraltar. Ceuta is a Spanish enclave in Morocco and we had to cross the border here, there is a large Arab presence with traditional tea shops and market squares.

Crossing over into Morocco we headed for Tangier with its beautiful beaches and street cafes, the markets were full of leather goods, carpets, jewellery, wood carvings, smells of lovely spices, the place full of noise and atmosphere. We bought our touristy silver bracelets for our families and all kinds of leather goods filling up the land rover, everything was so cheap. We headed into some remote places where the roads were very rough and neglected, often sand had blown across causing deep drifts, motor cars and heavy vehicles could not get through. We came across small convoys of vehicles just waiting for somebody with a shovel or such like to clear a path. The heat was almost unbearable when we turned up and started to tow the vehicles one by one through the sand drift. Most of the vehicle owners gave us a carton of cigarettes or a bottle of wine for our trouble. I was seriously thinking of staying a day or two because every time we had made a path through, the high wind blocked it again with the powder like sand. Finally we had enough and explored further into Morocco until we reached Rabat.

Camping for the night outside of a small remote village we had our tent up and a small campfire lit. Above us the black sky was speckled with millions of sparkling stars occasionally shooting stars shot across the heavens, I thought it the most beautiful sight I had ever witnessed. We broke open a bottle of good malt whiskey for a bed time nightcap, just then I thought how lucky we were to be there, when my parents had never even been abroad. The next morning after egg butties and coffee, we were packing up to go when two scrawny looking Arabs wondered into our camp. Before we could greet them they both pulled out a small knife then started to wave them aggressively in our faces obviously wanting to try intimidate and rob us. Taken by surprise I just stood still, my ex army pal picked up an axe from the back of our land rover and ran towards them shouting at them to "fuck off!" I have never seen anyone run away as fast, last we saw of them was two skinny Arabs clad in flowing ropes, hurtle towards the village. "Let's get going quick" shouted my mate, "they might be back with reinforcements shortly"! That was the only hairy moment in our whole trip, so we could not complain. They certainly were two ugly sods they looked like pantomime villains, I would not want to meet up with them again anytime soon!

My friend by this time wanted to return home to his girlfriend and when he phoned home from the next town, found out his job application for a career in the oil business had come good. So we reversed our course and headed home. I wondered what kind of work would come my way next. The sunshine and blue skies had been a nice contrast for me after the cold and rain of England it would take a bit of getting used to again. My trip through England, France, Spain and Morocco visiting out of the way remote places had been a lovely contrast to the years spent trawling up and down the Irish Sea. I was looking forward to seeing what would happen next.

CHAPTER EIGHTEEN

Home again and a diver friend asked me if I would be interested in a contract over the other side of Morecambe bay, helping his divers on the removal of the oil jetty, outside of Heysham harbour. Most of the jetty had already been removed and the concrete support bases had to be blown up down to below the level of the sea bottom. This was to avoid any obstructions on the seabed that could foul trawl nets or netting boats. This sounded a very interesting job opportunity so I quickly accepted his kind offer. I had to find a suitable boat that could carry four divers and their equipment plus bulky air compressors and needed it quick.

There were plenty of local men with suitable boats would love this contract. A thirty foot ex lifeboat that had come off a liner scrapped at Wards ship breakers came on the market I snapped it up straight away. She had a double diagonal hull, was very beamy and skilfully converted into a very strong workboat. A Perkins P6 diesel was fitted, you could tell all the work had been done by men who certainly knew what they were doing. My friend and I were very pleased with our purchase. My safari land rover was now surplus to requirements, my holiday was well and truly over, it was sold it and replaced with a Ford transit van to carry our equipment.

So our boat 'Margarita' loaded with four divers plus all their gear, made the first of several trips across Morecambe bay mooring up to the disused oil jetty just outside the port of Heysham. We spent several weeks tendering to our divers as they removed the last stumps of the piles until each remained under the seabed. Sometimes our boat got caught out in some terrible weather and received a bashing sailing across the bay. The divers informed us that in rough weather they would drive from Barrow in their vehicles and meet us in Heysham harbour, it had frightened them on some of the cross bay trips. The only unusual incident that happened on this charter was that one day as I rushed to unmoor the boat after a violent squall was screaming down the channel I lost my footing, falling head first into the boats cockpit, onto the air cylinders knocking myself unconscious. While the others were rushing around keeping the boat safe, I lay dead to the world and only came to when the boat was being moored up safely in Heysham dock. The headache lasted a hell of a long time but I still had to help bring the boat back to Barrow afterwards. Lucky it was my head that was injured anywhere else on my body might have been serious!

When this contract ended it was back to taking out angling clubs as the boat was not equipped for trawling. In order to skipper a charter boat each we purchased another boat similar to the Margarita, this new boat we named "Alco" and needed to install a new diesel engine in her. The two boats were booked up on a regular basis until the recession started to bite. Most of our regular clients were angling clubs from the factories around Wigan, Leyland and the mill towns. Our bookings became fewer as the factories closed down one after another, until it was not a feasible business anymore. All our adverts had to be cancelled in the angling magazines. At the peak of Barrow charter fishing there must have been a dozen boats working, most only booked for weekends. Also there were a good few angling charter boats working from Fleetwood, fishing alongside the Barrow lads, catching mostly quality plaice.

We tried working a set of trammel nets in the channel and across the bay, apart from regular plasters of jellyfish and star fish did not catch much. Seals were appearing in larger numbers in our area, in previous years only two or three would make their base on the south end of Walney Island. These few not being too much bother for us. Now they were getting cheeky and actively plundering our nets taking high value fish like bass and salmon out of the nets as we were pulling the nets aboard. We did not begrudge them a feed after all they have to survive. It was their habit of going along the nets taking one bite out of each fish belly that was annoying. This of course made our prime fish unsalable and made the difference of a wage to us. The fishermen today have to compete with a larger colony of seals numbering over one hundred that need a huge quantity of fish to survive so that the local fishermen cannot compete. We sold the Margareta to a local lad, the Alco was taken to Scotland on the Isle of Mull to collect and transport large quantities of winkles. The new owner wrote to me telling how well the boat was doing. That was the end of that chapter and another was just beginning.

CHAPTER NINETEEN

O ur friend Peter the shipping agent, suggested that we did a crewing job on a bucket dredger. This was contracted to dig a deep hole in the Walney channel, for the next nuclear submarine launch from Vickers shipbuilders. My first thought was amazement that there were any of these old vintage dredgers left afloat, my next was I thought Peter was a friend of ours! Being brought up in Barrow the inhabitants were used to the noise of bucket dredgers when the wind was westerly. Easterly winds meant the poor people who lived on Walney Island lost their sleep.

Talking to one of the deckhands on a bucket dredger about the noise he had to put up with he said "Think of the worst noise you have ever heard, it is nothing compared to being in close proximity to the screeching and howling on a bucket dredger. Metal against metal the noise is so bad the ear defenders are not adequate." The company after a lot of complaints from locals tried a 'silent link' bucket system without any success as I found out later.

A vintage steam dredger looks like a floating junkyard and is a stationary ship that needs to be towed by a tug from A to B. She is equipped with a continuous chain of steel buckets which carry through a structure called the ladder mounted on a U-shaped pontoon. The dredger is moored to six anchors, during dredging she swings around the bow anchor by taking in or paying out on the various steam winches aboard. The buckets which fill on the underside are emptied on the upper side by tipping their mud contents into a shute that empties into a spoil or hopper barge moored alongside. When the hopper barge is filled she casts off and sails to a designated dumping ground out to sea and returns for another load assuming in Barrow channels case there is enough water alongside the dredger when the tide is out. Since around the seventies bucket dredgers have nearly all been scrapped and replaced by trailing suction dredgers that operate like a hoover sucking up the mud and taking it out to dump. The other method is backhoe dredgers which drop spud legs to hold themselves in position and a hopper barge comes alongside, this method does not need anchors or wires laid out like the old dredgers, who were an obstruction to shipping channels, and have high maintenance cost, many highly skilled men are required and this is uneconomic. The modern methods are more efficient and cost effective.

My new role as deckhand was on the steam dredger 'Europe' this was owned by Westminster Dredging based then in Liverpool docks. Our job was to dig a very large deep hole for the newly built submarine to be launched into, as she slid into Walney channel. This usually went without a hitch except for an unfortunate nuclear submarine called 'Repulse.' She made worldwide fame when launched down the slips the tugs for various reasons did not get her towlines secured in time. Repulse had the ignominy to end up high and dry at low tide sitting on the mud, a major embarrassment for everyone involved. The film and pictures circulated all around the world. The towing company were never used again to my knowledge and the sub was swamped with officials inspecting for any damage. That was a never to be forgotten sight for Barrow people, a huge black leviathan beached at low tide like a stranded whale! Now that is what I call embarrassing.

Monday morning I turned up for work at the caravan used by the Westminster team for their site office, a quick handshake, no health and safety checks or inductions in those days. They informed me that a small powerful Beaver tug was waiting for me at the dock steps and to get a move on. The skipper like the rest of the dredger lads was a Scouser and that meant that he could piss take like the best of them. He looked about my age the first thing he did was pass me the wheel and started making us both a brew. "The Europe is berthed under the High Level Bridge in Devonshire dock waiting on us to tow her into the Anchorline basin, so best get a move on Norm." There was a speed limit in the dock so I had to be careful of our wash, when we were last in the dock with the Melanie Jane we made a wash that swept over a barge. This was manned by a squad of Vickers painters painting the side of a ship from scaffolding, they were not best pleased when their paint brushes and paint pots were washed overboard and they all got their feet wet. Steaming under the bridge the steam dredger Europe came into view, a heap of scrap metal with red rust stains running down her sides. Black smoke was pouring from her funnel pedestrians crossing the High Level Bridge were getting covered in sooty smuts. Her crew were swarming all over her getting the ship ready for her new charter. We pulled alongside and I coupled up the towline. The High Level Bridge started to lift, and with our engine at full power we started to get the huge dead weight of the dredger to move off the quay. When we had her lined up with the narrow gap of the bridge, the skipper gave me the wheel again and went to make us another brew.

Our tow rope was vibrating with the great strain of keeping this great mass of metal moving in a straight line and the sweat was dripping off me. My new friend the 'official' tug skipper sat in a chair with his feet up rolling a fag with seemingly not a care in the world. Looking upwards at the High Level Bridge I could see hundreds of people looking over at us, several buses held up by our passage no doubt feeling a bit disgruntled at our slow speed and the long delay. My Scouser friend said "They will have something to moan about if the bridge span gets stuck like it did the other day!" When we eventually got the dredger tied up in the Anchorline basin, I could meet the rest of the crew and the Europe's skipper, finding out some details about my job and hours. Most of the crew seemed like old men to me except for the dredger's skipper, he looked about my age. My hours on this contract were twelve hour shifts, seven days a week until the contract was finished.

We all chipped in for our food and each week had a set amount taken out of our wages. The old cook did wonders with our food, cooking a full English breakfast, two eggs, black pudding, fried bread the works, and later in the day a roast dinner followed by a pudding. This lovely food all served from a galley on the deck through a stable door. You collected your plate and carried it below quickly before the wind cooled it. The mess room was very basic a large wooden table with wood benches along either side. The meals were plentiful because it was hard manual work. The crew went ashore by tug at the end of their twelve hour shift to cheap hotel accommodation or digs, any local lads hired could go home.

This particular ancient dredger was built at Renfrew in 1955, you could tell she was not long for this world but somehow staggered on until 1983 when she was scrapped at Birkenhead. The other steam dredger I crewed on was 'Africa' built 1948 and sold for scrap in 1986. The Europe had two scotch boilers it was double stops ringing if a body or bomb came up in a bucket! After a few days of intense maintenance, greasing anything you could find with a five gallon drum of grease, getting wires spliced then rigged and a hundred other jobs done. We were at last ready to depart the dock system and head into Walney channel for Vickers slipway. The start of our contract to begin digging out the deep launching hole was to start in earnest.

The skipper of the beaver tug must have liked my big brown eyes he asked for me as deckhand again. A big cloud of black exhaust and full power applied, the great heap of scrap iron (I mean dredger) started her journey following behind our little tug like a dog on a lead. "Grab the wheel Norm I am going to put the kettle on and roll myself a fag." A bit of a pattern was emerging here, but what the hell he was the skipper, but the idea of towing this dredger out of the dock entrance and up channel to the shipyard in a four knot current was to say the least rather daunting. One thing was clear I did not need to have much power on when the tide was flowing our way. A mug of tea was shoved in my hand the skipper put his feet up on the instrument panel and started reading the Sun newspaper. "Look at the tits on her Norm I would like to give her one." The launching slips were coming up fast and I was starting to sweat profusely. "Do you want to take the wheel now skipper we are nearly in position I think?"

"No your doing fine Norm" without even lifting his head out of the news paper. Just when a voice in my head said this is going to be a disaster, the Europe sounded her horn and must have dropped her anchor, then all forward movement ceased, thank goodness. If her anchor had not held straight away she would have crashed into Jubilee Bridge causing millions of pounds of damage, I would have never been hired at sea ever again. My skipper was either the coolest sailor ever or a complete nut job.

Bucket dredgers over many years had laid out permanent mooring points on each side of the Barrow shipping channel, to save time many old ships anchors had been dug in. Heavy chain and wire cables ran down to the channel edge so that the little tug could run out the dredger's own cables, and shackle up quickly then dredging could commence. The tugs had steps cut into the stem and little draught forward so the crew could climb down and shackle up the wires on the beach. This was graft dragging the wires up the beach to marry them up, not a popular job in a howling gale and rain in the middle of the night. Before any dredging work we would go with the surveyor to put up several marker post painted bright orange for seeing in daylight, flashing lights were attached to see at night. We used a sextant which showed the dredger skipper how far to dredge forwards and sideways because the company only got paid for the depth and area of the cut needed, any spoil taken away unnecessarily would not be paid for by the Ministry of Defence. These days GPS systems are used not sextants.

The harbour authority had the job of surveying the area before, during and after, to make sure the right area and depth was correct, using their new survey boat 'Dova Haw'. Little did I know then, that in the future I would be the skipper in charge of that new painted all white survey boat! The dredging company also used the beaver tug to survey it themselves, as a double check. What with work on the tug and operating the starboard side steam winch they got their money's worth out of me. Most spoil hoppers were quite ugly box like ships but the two that worked on our contract were more like small coasters, they were bonnie looking vessels called 'Tyne' and 'Clyde'.

The hoppers were alongside and the ladder was dropped to the seabed, the endless bucket chain started to chew into the silt and full buckets rose out of the water to cascade down the shute into the hopper. Before we actually started to dredge I had a brush with death, my mate was on the winch lifting the spud a touch, so I could pull out the retaining pin that held the spud in the air. The two spuds were used to lower the aft end side wires under the water to allow the hopper barges to come alongside, without having their propellers snagged by the side wires. He lifted the heavy spud with the winch and I was standing with the heavy pin in my hand. There was a loud crack! The spud fell, the girder with the pulley on actually grazed the tip of my nose as it whistled past my face. My mate was as white has a sheet and I was in shock, sitting down realising how close a call that was. The skipper and engineer had seen what happened and quickly checked to see why it had broken off, the culprit being the welder, he had only tack welded the girder in position and completely forgotten to finish it off properly. The skipper said to me "Go and have a sit down for ten minutes Norm and grab a cup of tea."

That was the last I heard about it, the girder was welded back and dredging commenced. Things would be a little different nowadays that is for sure.

The noise off the buckets being metal to metal was excruciating, even to try and hear the skipper in his small control cabin ringing his brass bell to tell you when to start heaving or letting out on your winch was very difficult to hear. When the cut was starting, the bell would tell you to start heaving to your starboard side, when the skipper rang it again you stopped your winch hauling and let the wire run out slowly. The port winch man would then start his winch, hauling the dredger back until the bell told him to stop again, in the mean time the skipper would have winched the dredger forward a little each time to start a fresh cut. It could get very confusing with the constant noise from the dredger and the hoppers tied alongside, the water or rocks falling out of the buckets going up the ladder and crashing onto the roof of the small shelter that the winch was housed under. You would think you heard the bell and start hauling and it was not the bell you heard, the other winch was still hauling and the wire cables would crack under the tug of war going on, I would have kittens and realise my mistake before a wire broke with dangerous consequences.

It was easy to make mistakes when you are all tired and ready for home. Often under the strain of pulling the weight of a dredger and two hopper barges it would cause the side wire to snap, then we would jump on to the tug and run another wire out as quickly as possible. Another hard job was lifting the dredger's huge heavy forward anchor and tying it off the tug's starboard quarter with a heavy strop. Then with a hell of a list on the beaver tug, take it up tide and drop it in a new position. This dredging contract was made worse by the continuous heavy snow blowing in our faces and constant gales. This particular night we were on the deck frozen and blue with cold, we finally got both hoppers filled and away before low water. Unfortunately a side wire snapped so I got dropped ashore by the tug to couple up a new wire in the dark, both my wellies were full of water and my feet frozen, back on board my hands and fingers were blue. Luckily the skipper let us go below for a couple of hour's shelter before the next shift arrived on the tug from Barrow.

The surveys showed that the required cubic tons of silt had been removed and we towed the Europe back into Barrow docks, and spent a few days decommissioning the dredger, ready for the sea voyage to her next contract. We were thinking that this would be like a holiday working inside the docks. We tied up the dredger and were all sat in the mess room having a brew when the skipper walked in "Who would like a cushy job with double pay, if so put your hand up!" Quicker than you could say "Mugs" my mate put his hand up followed a split second later by me. Looking round with a smug expression on our faces we could see everyone else pissing themselves laughing. "What is so funny?" I said. The skipper said "You will know soon enough go and report to the engineer he will kit you out for boiler cleaning, it will be the last time you ever volunteer for this job!" Heading along the deck towards the engine room I was thinking how shitty can boiler cleaning be at double time it cannot be that bad.

How my illusions were soon to be shattered, it would be the first and last time I would ever put myself anywhere near the front of a Scotch boiler. The grumpy ancient engineer handed us a pair of goggles, face mask, gloves, stack of large bags, wire brushes, brush and shovel. He explained that the boiler was honey combed, with lots of V- shaped metal rods inside called diffusers I think. We had to pull each rod out and clean the soot off, then clean out the hole of soot residue, problem was the boiler had not yet cooled down properly and the heat was still there. The soot was like fine talcum powder and got everywhere, we sweated and the soot stuck, it seeped through the vent holes in the goggles into our eyes, it even got through our face mask. Every now and again we coughed up a rather large soot ball.

This job was really the pits we both agreed when we went onto the deck for a breath of fresh air, black as chimney sweeps. The rest of the deck lads were sauntering around with grease guns greasing anything that did not move or stowing away wire and ropes, having a good laugh. At last all of the soot had been bagged up including our boiler suits, anything that had come into contact with the soot disposed of. The engineer and skipper said we had done such a good job we could do it again on the next boiler clean, my answer was unprintable. The next contract was crewing on the steam dredger Africa which was even older than the Europe needless to say I did not volunteer to do any boiler cleaning.

CHAPTER TWENTY

About this time I thought I would try selling fish from a van full time and cut out the middle man. So in the early hours of the morning would set off for Fleetwood fish market to buy my own fish. Mostly I bought cod, coley or hake landed that morning from the deep sea Icelandic trawlers. Then dash back along the motorway to get back to Barrow for lunchtime, in order to catch the shipyard workers coming out of the gates for lunch. My old pensioner friend used to help me by cutting the huge fillets up into one pound steaks and bagging them up at fifty pence a bag. They and the boxes of Manx kippers and yellow smoked haddock would sell like hot cakes. Some of our customers bought ten bags a time for their freezer. The bus depot was another good place to visit in those days, there were still plenty of factories in Barrow and we would soon sell out of fish. We had a visit one day from the environment health officer who said I needed to have washing facilities in my vehicle and a hawkers licence. Thinking in for a penny in for a pound it was time to invest in a custom made mobile fish van duly ordered from a garage in York.

The van looked a treat a bowler hat on a cod with a walking stick and various crab/ lobster characters made it look very colourful, too attractive, every time I pulled up anywhere kids would come up to the cab asking for ice creams! The large fitted sliding window was great for serving customers. Also installed inside was a hot water boiler and stainless steel sinks for washing hands. The van was a brand new Commer van that would pass any health inspection and should, it cost a bloody fortune. When I arrived early morning in Fleetwood fish market there must have been fifty other fish vans, most were wrecks setting out to all the towns in the North West to sell their fish. Obviously they were not being bothered by any health officials. I would not personally buy any fish off that lot they looked like mobile skips and some of the drivers looked more like vagrants. Eventually I built up a loyal clientele in our surrounding district but really missed catching them myself. After a while somebody made me a fair offer for my business so I sold up.

CHAPTER TWENTY ONE

My lifelong friend Brian built a steel thirty foot trawler and charter boat single handed on a rented piece of land next to Ferry beach. This boat was a cracker and had a forward wheelhouse with deep aft cockpit for angling parties to fish safely in rough seas. He fished it successfully for a long time and one day knowing I was missing fishing invited me into another partnership with him in his boat 'Westward'. We laid her up for a complete refit at Ferry beach which took several weeks. After many hours of hard work she was painted up and ready for launching. We dragged her into position using chain blocks and had her pointing bow down on the old cobbled ferry pitching facing Walney channel. Westward was tied off with a stout rope that stopped her rushing down the steep pitching.

This is when Brian and I had our first disagreement. He wanted to wait until the tide was in later that day and lower her gently into the water very slowly, using the chain blocks to stop her running away out of control. Of course being impulsive and having no patience what so ever, I wanted to cut the rope holding her straight away. Then watch her slide down the slope seeing how far nearer the tide she would end up. My thinking was this would be saving us a lot of time. To his credit Brian said the boat being seven tons would go down the slope like a rocket if the rope was cut, but if I wanted to be an impatient smart arse to go ahead and sever the rope.

They say pride comes before a fall, cutting the rope one strand at a time I realised Brian might have been right, the stress on the rope was too much, before I could change my mind the last strand of rope parted. With a mighty crack it parted causing a heap of onlookers to throw themselves in all directions to avoid being squashed!

The Westward all seven tons of highly painted steel shot off like an Exocet missile towards the channel, bouncing off several boats of various descriptions that stood in her way. The sounds were frightening, metal keel racing down the slippery granite cobbles, sparks flying everywhere. Finally she was brought up suddenly by hitting a smart yacht, pushing it three feet bodily out of her way, splintering several feet of the yacht's highly varnished teak belting. After all that noise, suddenly you could hear a pin drop! Total silence, everyone picked themselves up off the floor and stared at the Westward only a few yards off the water.

Brian looked at me and said "I do not believe you have just done that, you bloody nutter, the repairs to that yacht and any other damage are coming out of your pocket!" and walked away shaking his head.

We had a successful contract with the Customs and Excise to go on patrol up and down the coastline, boarding ships and small boats to show a Customs presence, a job which at times could be very interesting. We got on great with the two officers that usually went with us and our coffee was always laced liberally with rum. We had our flag flying proudly whilst on patrol, the Westward looking the part painted up like a yacht. The custom officers looked very smart in uniform and white caps. They had a good tip off ensuring us dashing out one early morning heading for the port of Whitehaven several miles up the coast to board an incoming ship. Heading past the entrance to the Duddon estuary we strayed onto the dangerous bar, which over the winter had built up much further seawards than usual, our keel touched on and the boat stopped suddenly. Quick as a flash a wave towered over us sweeping into our open cockpit. I knew that if we could not put our bow into the next wave, the next one would fill up our vulnerable open cockpit and we could founder.

Quickly pushing the throttle fully open for maximum power and the wheel hard over, the bow seemed to be taking forever to come around into the next wave. This next wave was already beginning to tower over us. Glancing out of the wheelhouse door to check on our Customs officers I could see them both swilling about in three feet of water in the cockpit, their white hats floating away. Somebody as usual was keeping an eye on us that day the bow came around at the same time as the next wave thundered past. A couple of times the keel hit the bar before we reached deeper water and safety. The senior officer entered the wheelhouse minus his hat saying in a quiet voice "Forget the patrol Norm, take us home!"

The work we did for the Customs was varied and exciting, some of which we did cannot be talked about. Our last assignment was to show some new officers the short cut through the North end of Walney channel, which is tricky you need to know the right states of tide and correct depths to navigate safely. This tuition was for when they bought a boat of their own to patrol the coast line except for a few odd call outs we had finished our work with them for good. Another interesting charter the Westward did was for a chase boat for a company surveying Morecambe bay and the waters off Barrow for gas and oil deposits. Our job was to warn off other shipping coming too close to the survey vessel interfering with their work. The survey was very successful, gas was found off the coast of Barrow and the gas rigs have been supplying gas ever since.

CHAPTER TWENTY TWO

Following the drowning of a number of local people in the Duddon estuary during 1969, a public meeting was held in our village Askam-in- Furness, on the shore of this beautiful but dangerous estuary. A decision was taken to start a village own quick response rescue service to operate in the Duddon estuary, Roanhead sand dunes and the North end of Walney Island. This rescue service is a voluntary organisation dedicated to the rescue or assistance of anyone or anything in peril from the sea in our area, its twenty eight miles of shoreline encloses an area of thirteen square miles making it the second largest estuary in Cumbria. The channels and gully's change every week, depth and location forever changing, due to high tides and heavy rainfall bringing large quantities of fresh water flowing in from the various rivers. Areas of sinking sand appear one day and are gone the next. Since fund raising all those years ago to buy the first inflatable and tractor to launch our boat, the incidents attended have been over four hundred, in and around the treacherous waters of our estuary. Some call outs have been very frustrating others mundane, and some heart warming where lives have been saved. Alas some are tragic where in spite of the best efforts of all concerned life has been lost.

Most of the original trustees of the Duddon Inshore Rescue have passed away and recently we lost our chairman Bernard McNamee MBE who spent a great part of his life making sure that the local lifeboat is always on station ready. All the crew highly trained and kitted out to a professional standard. His son Christopher and family also the rest of the many volunteers work tirelessly to keep the station going, only managing by the goodwill of the local community to fund raise enough money during the year. A local man donated some land for the new extension of the boathouse and local businesses are generous, enabling the lifeboat service to carry on year after year independent of funding from official sources. When the boathouse is used by the various different agencies such as the coastguards, police and other volunteer organisations to coordinate a rescue in the estuary sandwiches and hot drinks are supplied by the villagers. A donation from each book sold will go to Duddon Inshore Rescue in the hope that we can carry on for many years to come.

CHAPTER TWENTY THREE

The view now looking out to sea from our favourite boyhood camping site at Thorny Nook on Walney Island, would shock the long gone old timers who taught me my boating skills. Mile after mile of towering windmills row after row blotting out the horizon. Covering our rich fishing and prawn grounds where we used to happily trawl up and down day after day. Some people say this is progress, many say that they are a blot on our beautiful coastline. If I had to pick where they were to be sited land or sea I would pick sea, the lesser of two evils. I believe that our beautiful country is too small to be blighted with rows of giant windmills dominating our lovely landscape.

Over the years our camping place on the island has been gradually washed away by the sea leaving no trace of the original site. Overlooking our Ferry Beach is an enormous shipbuilding shed called Devonshire Dock Hall, so huge it can be seen from Blackpool promenade over twenty miles away. This hall was built in 1986 for Vickers using part of Devonshire dock, infilling with over two million tons of sand pumped in from nearby Roosecote sands where we would set our bank lines all those years ago. It provides for the sheltered conditions to build surface vessels or submarines in a much safer environment than the exposed old fashioned slipways. No more Vickers craftsmen working in rain and freezing winds on the exposed slipways under the cover of a flimsy canvas. Or us boatmen risking life and limbs rescuing launch timbers from the rip tides of Walney channel working off flimsy converted ships lifeboat.

In front of the hall is a 24,300 tonne capacity ship lift to enable completed vessels to be lowered into the calm dock independently of time and tides. This is also used to lift vessels out of the dock to take into the hall for refits. The ship lift was the largest in the world on completion and first used for the launch of the Trident class of submarine, which were called the Vanguard, Victorious, Vigilant and Vengeance. The shipyard is currently building the Astute class of submarines and hopefully for the security of our shipyard the next generation of Trident submarines. An amazing contrast to the sound of riveters and caulkers hammers that we went to sleep listening to every night, when as children were tucked up safely in bed, all those years ago in Glasgow Street!

GLOSSARY

Amidships	Mid section of vessel
Aft	Stern section of a boat
Abeam	To come level with another vessel
Bar	Build up of sand across river or estuary
Beam	Width of vessel across the deck at widest point
Stays	Wire supporting mast
Baulks	Large pieces of timber
Belay	Make fast or tie off
Bend on	Tie two ropes together
Bight	A loop in rope
Bilge	Bottom of a boat in the mid section
Bitter end	Very end of a coil of rope
Bridles	Part of the rigging of a trawl net
Bulwarks	The extension of the hull above the deck to stop crew or gear going overboard
Bulkhead	A partition on a boat sometimes water tight
Butt	Formed by two planks meeting end to end on a frame
Cabin sole	Cabin floor
Capstan	Mechanical device to haul ropes and cable
Carvel	A planking method where planks lay edge to edge

Caulking	Seams of planks packed with waterproof material to prevent leaking
Cleat	A device for securing a rope
Clinker	A method of planking on a boat where plank edges overlap
Coamings	A frame around a deck opening usually 6 to 12 inches higher than the deck itself
Cod end knot	Quick release knot that when pulled releases the bag of fish
Cod end	The very end of a trawl net where the catch gathers
Dahn	A buoy used to mark the end of a net, long line, Or fleet of crab pots. Marker flag attached
Deck wash	Sea water pumped to a hose pipe on the deck
Drag	To tow a trawl
Draught	Depth of hull from waterline to keel
Fairlead	A guide to keep rope in position over a boat's rail
Fathom	Six feet
Footrope	A heavy rope with chain wrapped around the the bottom half of a trawl mouth to make contact with the seabed
Forepeak	Small cabin in the bow of a boat
Frames	The inside skeleton of a vessel that carry planks usually made from oak
Gallows	To hang the otter boards from
Gunnels	The top outside rail of a boat
Headrope	Top upper rope of a trawl

Hitch	A type of knot
Heads	Toilet
Jib	Triangular sail set between masthead and bowsprit
Keel	Heavy oak or elm baulk forming the back bone of a boat
Knot	Speed of a vessel through the water based on a nautical mile of 2000yards
Lanyard	Length of rope tied to a fender or bucket
Lee	Downwind
Leg	A stout timber shaped to fit midships on the vessel to hold boat upright when tide leaves the boat in drying harbour
Mizzen	Aft mast sail
Otter boards	Devices for keeping the trawl net spread when towing behind the boat
Deck boards	Boards 8 to 12 inches in height set fore and aft to prevent catch sliding about
Quarters	The port and starboard aft sections of a boat
Rail	The reinforced timber around the top of the boats hull
Rudder	Steering device at the stern of a boat
Scuppers	The gap between the deck and bulwarks for drainage of seawater

Port	Left side vessel looking forward
Starboard	Right hand of vessel looking forward
Sidewinders	Trawlers that shoot their trawls over the side, stern trawlers over the stern
Spell	A rest or taking a break
Stem	The very front of boat linking keel to Deck and carrying the plank ends
Stern post	The oak post linking keel to deck carrying the transom or if double ender the plank ends
Transom	The flat stern of the vessel
Warps	Rope trawl warps or steel wire running from trawlers winch to the seabed to tow the trawl net
Yarn	To talk or tell a story

Names of fishing boats owned or part owned over the years

Provider
Mischief
Misty Morn
Fruitful
Meteor
Easter Morn
Melanie Jane
Bonnie Lou
Silver Spray
Sula
Alco
Margarita
Jane
Westward
Saltaire
Yachts
Ann Doreen
Pauline